Praise for
LIVE SMART AFTER 50!

"Who do you want to become now and how will you make it happen? Read LIVE SMART AFTER 50! *You may discover your answers."*

— Jane Pauley, Emmy-award-winning journalist and AARP host of TODAY show's *Your Life Calling*

"This book reveals powerful and purposeful practices for living an authentic, smart life. Don't pass 50 without it!"

— Richard Leider, bestselling author of *The Power of Purpose* and *Repacking Your Bags*

"This book is a terrific resource. It's the right book at the right time."

— Ken Dychtwald, Ph.D., author of *Age Wave* and *A New Purpose: Redefining Money, Family, Work, Retirement and Success*

"An informative and practical guide... including valuable insights on caregiving."

— Leisa Easom for Rosalynn Carter

"This practical and thorough guide has the rare ability to take the uncertainty of the future into consideration while simultaneously deepening hope and the potential for mastery. It represents the next generation of self-help primers. One to read and to keep close by."

— Carol Orsborn, Ph.D., Author of *Fierce with Age: Chasing God and Squirrels in Brooklyn*

*"*LIVE SMART AFTER 50! *speaks to Boomers in their language, focusing on progress, reflective thinking and choices. A good read for anyone."*

— Mary Bleiberg, President, ReServe

"The great strength and wisdom of this book lies in its multiple approaches and mind sets. This book is a gold mine. You can be the wise miner."

— George H. Schofield, Ph.D., author of *After 50 It's Up To Us: Developing the Skills and Agility We'll Need*

"*Muddling is out. Planning is in. Who do you want to be in this next stage of your life? This book offers spot-on advice and inspiration to help all of us plan, prepare, and smoothly navigate this new frontier.*"

— Kerry Hannon, award-winning author of *AARP Great Jobs for Everyone 50+: Finding Work That Keeps You Happy and Healthy ... And Pays the Bills* and *What's Next? Follow Your Passion and Find Your Dream Job*

"*The Experts at LPN in* LIVE SMART AFTER 50! *are pioneers ... Phenomenal, practical and enabling... Amazing piece that touches my heart, myself and my clients. ...* "

— Terri Hilliard Olson, Esq., Estate and Senior counselor at law in Westlake Village, CA

"*Written by perceptive experts in aging and life transitions, this guide is an insightful read with guidance for self-reflection and practical tips... We should all read it, at any age.*"

— Katrina Rogers, Ph. D., Senior Vice President, Fielding Graduate University and Conference Leader, the Fourth and Fifth Annual International Conference on Positive Aging

"*This short book is just amazing. It can be a life-saving, handy reference to use along the way. If you're smart, you'll want to get this book, keep it handy and give copies to those you care about.*"

— William A. Sadler, Ph.D., Sociologist and author of *The Third Age: Six Principles of Growth and Renewal after Forty* and *Changing Course: Navigating Life after 50* (with James Krefft)

"*This book wows me. Thorough, generous and content rich — at last a guide to navigating these years with some ease, joy and peace of mind.*"

— Leah Komaiko, Brand Consultant and author of *Am I Old Yet?*

"*Who among us hasn't found themselves lost and needing directions in a strange place? Earlier guidelines no longer work. We need a GPS to help us find our way in new territory, and* LIVE SMART AFTER 50! *is exactly the guidance system we need. Don't leave home without it!*"

— Harry R. Moody, Ph.D., Vice President and Director of Academic Affairs, AARP

"This guide from the Life Planning Network is an invaluable companion to figuring out what's next. From work to civic engagement, housing to health, this book will help you live your legacy, rather than just leave one."
— Marc Freedman, Founder and CEO of Encore.org

"At last — a fantastic practical handbook for finding your way in work, play and love as you head into the new bonus years after midlife. LIVE SMART AFTER 50! is like a loyal friend who is understanding, supportive and full of good advice."
— Abigail Trafford, author of *My Time: Making the Most of the Bonus Decades after 50* and *As Time Goes By: Boomerang Marriages, Serial Spouses, Throwback Couples and Other Romantic Adventures in an Age of Longevity.*

"The authors of LIVE SMART AFTER 50! come from diverse backgrounds and perspectives. They're united in offering practical suggestions and philosophical guideposts for navigating the journey of a longer life. Keep this book around. You'll want to refer to it over the years."
— Chris Farrell, author of *The New Frugality: How to Consume Less, Save More, and Live Better*

"This readable volume is chock full of practical advice on how to stay engaged and productive through the longer lives we'll be living. The first step in planning for a longer, healthier, more productive life is to read this book."
— John W. Rowe , M.D., Chairman, MacArthur Network on an Aging Society, Professor of Health Policy and Management, Mailman School of Public Health, Columbia University, co-author of *Successful Aging*

"This volume brings together the experiences and wisdom of experts who work with individuals entering this new stage of life. Of particular value are the exercises, activities, and tools for people who are looking for a self-guided tour through the 50s and beyond or for individuals who are helping others navigate this new stage of life. Everyone will find benefit in reading this book regardless of age or occupation."
— Lois Tetrick, Professor of Psychology at George Mason University and Director of the Industrial and Organizational Psychology Program

"Some coaches give great pep talks; others provide great playbooks. The Life Planning Network's experts do both in LIVE SMART AFTER 50*! Read it and put together a game plan for the life you want to live."*

— James S. Kunen, author of *Diary of a Company Man: Losing a Job, Finding a Life*

"This wise and useful book titles itself 'a guide to life planning' yet I see it more as a conversation with wise and experienced individuals. They offer their information and experience along with their wisdom and encouragement to help you, as you age, to explore your possibilities for growth."

— Connie Goldman, author of *Who Am I ... Now That I'm Not Who I Was?*, *The Gifts of Caregiving*, and *Late-Life Love*

"A stellar cadre of experts present a clear and compelling overview of life planning in contemporary times for those in midlife and beyond. Evidence-based and practical, the book empowers those motivated to take action in the midst of the unknown."

— Connie Corley, Professor, Fielding Graduate University and Host / Producer, "Experience Talks" radio show on KPFK-FM

LIVE SMART AFTER 50!

The Experts' Guide to Life
Planning for Uncertain Times

LPN Editorial Board

Natalie Eldridge, Chair

Doug Dickson

Bruce Frankel

Andrea Gallagher

Meg Newhouse

Mary Radu

LIFE PLANNING NETWORK
Boston, Massachusetts

Ordering Information:
Quantity sales. Special discounts are available on quantity purchases by corporations, associations, and others. For details, contact the publisher at the following email address: Orders@LiveSmartAfter50.com

Website: www.LiveSmartAfter50.com

Library of Congress Control Number: 2012948945
Paperback - 978-0-9881907-0-2
eBook - 978-0-9881907-1-9

Manufactured in the United States of America

2 4 6 8 9 7 5 3

First Edition

While Life Planning Network has made every effort to provide accurate telephone numbers and Internet addresses at the time of publication, neither it, the editors nor the contributors assume any responsibility for errors, or for changes that occur after publication. Further, the publisher does not have any control over and does not assume any responsibility for contributor or third-party websites or their content.

This book is dedicated to positive aging pioneers
Dr. Gene Cohen and Dr. Robert Butler,
who changed the focus on aging from problems to potential
and its image from decline to creativity.

And to all the men and women over fifty
who show us how to age by continuing to contribute
to their families, communities and the world
with their experience, wisdom and courage.

 Contents

Acknowledgments

No book is born without a vision, a passion, a plan and the support of many people. The Life Planning Network would like to thank all of its members, from whose expertise and energy this book arose. We especially thank Carleen MacKay, who first envisioned this book and, along with Andrea Gallagher, convinced us to embark on the journey. Our deepest gratitude goes to Natalie Eldridge, who conducted the symphony of thirty-three authors in composing this unique work and also led the tireless efforts of the Editorial Board — Doug Dickson, Bruce Frankel, Andrea Gallagher, Meg Newhouse and Mary Radu — in "growing" the book and shaping the content, tone and underlying themes. A special thanks to Paula Cole, whose expert editing improved the continuity, flow and accessibility for the reader. We offer an appreciative bow to each of the Chapter Leaders and Contributors for the rich, dynamic and wise content they provided.

Creating a useful roadmap was not enough. We needed to get our book into the hands of men and women looking for a way to better navigate life after 50. A special thank you to the Marketing Team, led by Bruce Frankel, Mary Radu and Andrea Gallagher and including Doug Dickson, Viki Kind, Barbara Meltzer, Dorian Mintzer, Fred Mandell, and Roberta Taylor, for their creative efforts in reaching out to our endorsers and our readers, and to Eileen Caroscio and the National Communications Team for their efforts reaching out to our members and the media. We extend our gratitude to Cynthia Frank at Cypress House Publishing who was an invaluable guide in creating this book.

Much appreciation to Max Schwear, for his fresh and spirited artistry in creating the cover design for our book and to Lee Abel for contributing many of the photo portraits used in the book. We also extend our thanks to Jim Montalto, Doug Smith and Penne Baer for web and administrative support.

Special thanks to the following individuals for their contributions to the book:

To Joan who shared her moving story in the Well-Being for Life chapter; to attorneys Claire A. DeMarco and Tovah Poster who contributed to the Your Wishes Matter chapter and to Carol Anderson, Michael Smith, and John Nelson for their contributions to the Bring Meaning to Money chapter.

Finally, The Life Planning Network would like to thank all the people who shared their stories with the authors, and to the warm support of our families, friends, and clients.

 # Contributors

Barbara Abramowitz, M Ed, LMHC, LMFT, Licensed Psychotherapist and Certified Body-Mind Life Coaching™ Specialist, www.optimallivingnow.com.

Bradley T. Baumann, CFP®, Certified Financial Planner™, Sudden Money® Advisor, www.BradBaumann.com. (Chapter Co-Leader)

Bill Brisk, JD, PhD, Elder Law Attorney, Editor-In-Chief of the National Association of Elder Law Attorneys Journal, www.briskelderlaw.com. (Chapter Leader)

Elizabeth Craig, MBA, MCDP, CCM, Master Career and Job Search Strategist, Speaker and Consultant, www.elcglobal.com.

Helen Dennis, MA, Specialist in aging, employment and the new retirement, Co-author of *Project Renewment: The First Retirement Model for Career Women.* (Chapter Leader)

Doug Dickson, President, Discovering What's Next, www.discoveringwhatsnext.com. (Chapter Leader)

Kendall Dudley, MA, Career and Life Design Consultant, www.kendalldudley.com.

Natalie Eldridge, PhD, Psychologist and Life Transition Coach, Author of *Action on Purpose* Newsletter, www.EldridgeWorks. com.

Bruce Frankel, Author of *What Should I Do With the Rest of My Life? True Stories of Finding Success, Passion and New Meaning in the Second Half of Life,* www.brucefrankel.net.

Judith-Kate Friedman, Author of "The Songwriting Works ™ Model" in Hartman-Stein & LaRue, *Enhancing Cognitive Fitness in Adults,* Springer, 2011, www.Songwritingworks.org.

Andrea Gallagher, Certified Senior Advisor, President Senior Concerns, 2011-2012 President of Life Planning Network (LPN). www.seniorconcerns.org. (Chapter Co-Leader)

Sara Zeff Geber, PhD, Certified Retirement Options Coach, President of LifeEncore®, Author of *Fifty Plus, Minus Kids: Navigating Later Life without Adult Children,* www.LifeEncore. com.

Joanne Hadlock, EdD, NCCC, Counseling Psychologist, Nationally Certified Career Consultant, www.joannehadlock.us.

Dick Haid, PhD, PCC, Adult Mentor, www.adultmentor.com.

Kit Harrington Hayes, MEd, Founder and Principal of LifeWork Design, Author of *Managing Career Transitions,* www.KitHayes.com. (Co-Chapter Leader)

Jan Hively, PhD, Co-founder of the Vital Aging Network, www.vital-aging-network.org, the Minnesota Creative Arts and Aging Network, www.mncaan.net, and the SHiFT Network, www.shiftonline.org.

Margaret "Peggy" Hothem, EdD, Professor of Leisure and Recreational Studies, Gordon College, www.Gordon.edu.

Elizabeth W. Jetton, CFP®, Financial Planner, Consultant and Educator, www.DirectionsforWomen.com, www.ElizabethJetton. com. (Chapter Co-Leader)

Karma Kitaj, PhD, Certified Life Coach, Psychotherapist, Artist, Author of *Women Who Could… and Did: Stories of 26 Exemplary Artists & Scientists,* www.LifeSpringCoaching.com, www.RetirementAsYouWantIt.com. (Chapter Leader)

Donna Krone, CPCC, Certified True Purpose™ Coach/Facilitator, www.sacredconversations.com.

Moira Lanier, Founder, President and Master Trainer, Greatest Age Fitness, Inc., www.greatestagefitness.com. (Chapter Leader)

Carleen MacKay, Director Mature Workforce Initiatives, Career Partners International. Author of *Plan "B" for Boomers, The 50,000 Mile Checkup*, and *WORK* (in press). Co-author of *Return of the Boomers, Boom or Bust*, and *Myth Cards*, www.agelessinamerica.com. (Chapter Leader)

Fred Mandell, PhD, Creative Catalyst, Artist and co-author of *Becoming a Life Change Artist: 7 Creative Skills to Reinvent Yourself at Any Stage of Life*, www.fredmandell.com.

Dorian Mintzer, MSW, PhD, BCC, Life Transition/Retirement Coach, Founder of Boomers and Beyond Special Interest Group, Co author of *The Couples Retirement Puzzle*, www.revolutionizeretirement.com, www.couplesretirementpuzzle.com.

Margaret (Meg) Newhouse, PhD, CPCC, (Certified Life Coach), Author of *Life Planning for the Third Age*, www.passionandpurpose.com. (Chapter Leader)

Ron Pevny, MA, Life Coach, Certified Sage-ing Leader, Founder of the Center for Conscious Eldering, www.centerforconsciouseldering.com.

Mary Radu, MS, MSW, CPCC, Certified Professional Coach, Philanthropy Mentor and author of the *The Roadmap to Meaningful Midlife*®, www.pathmakercoaching.com.

Renee Lee Rosenberg, MA, LMHC, Author of *Achieving the Good Life After 50: Tools and Resources for Making It Happen*, Certified Five O'Clock Club Master Coach and Retirement Specialist, www.retirementutor.com, www.positivitypro.com.

Donna Schempp, LCSW, Family Caregiver Alliance, Consultant, dschempp@att.net.

Paula K. Solomon, MSSW, Life Coach specializing in life transitions and helping caregivers maintain well-being, www.TheSeasonsofYourLife.com.

Candy Spitz, LCSW, ACC, Career & Life Coach, www.boomerslifecoach.com.

Roberta K. Taylor, RNCS, MEd, Certified Senior Advisor, Life Planning/Retirement Coach, Co-author of *The Couple's Retirement Puzzle*, www.pathmaking.com, www.couplesretirementpuzzle.com. (Chapter Leader)

Chuck Yanikoski, Retirement Adviser, www.ChuckYRetirement.com. (Chapter Co-Leader)

 Preface

"The times they are a-changin'" — Bob Dylan

BOB DYLAN'S LEGENDARY ANTHEM from the 1960s talks about the cultural and political changes of that time. But the sentiment applies as much to our lives today as it did to those earlier events. Things continue to change in ways that affect us all.

This comes as no surprise. Technology, the global economy, a shifting job market, political uncertainty—together, they create a backdrop of change that colors our options as we look to the future.

Aging in a Changing World

Aging is only part of the challenge we face. Frederick Lynch, in his book, *One Nation under AARP*, says, "Aging boomers will grow old in a new society. The taken-for-granted economic, political, and cultural order is rapidly changing." This requires that we shift our attitudes, learn new skills and open our eyes to new possibilities, adding to the complexity of midlife transitions in the early 21st century.

And, by now, it's quite clear that each of us, as individuals, is changing. In addition to differences in how we look and how we feel, our sense of who we are and what's important shifts as we age. These changes come from both inside and out.

Internal changes may poke at us for a while before we start to pay attention. But they come to the surface at key moments and push us to think differently about who we are and what we want or need.

Do any of these thoughts sound familiar?

- Work just doesn't feel as satisfying or challenging as it once did.

- Wouldn't it be great to take a few months off to (fill in the blank)?

- What do I really want to do when (or if) I'm able to retire?

- I want to help my aging parents (or adult kids ... or both), but when will I have time for the things I want to do as well?

- I've been so busy, I feel like I've lost touch with the people and causes I care about.

- I want to do something more purposeful, more meaningful with my life.

This is hardly a complete list, but it suggests some of the feelings many of us begin to have as we reach our 50s, 60s and 70s.

Changes also come from the outside. Shifts in health or family circumstance, loss of a loved one or a job — events like these can force people to ask, "What's next for me?"

One change in particular affects all of us living in the second half of our lives (roughly age 50 and beyond). It's a change that's new and unique to our generation and those that will follow ours. We all know that the average age of the population is creeping upward every year. Increasing longevity is opening up an entirely new life stage, one that fits between midlife and old age, and it can span 20 or 30 years.

During this new stage, most people will continue to be healthy, active and engaged. It doesn't have a label yet, but some have referred to this stage as the "bonus" years (Abigail Trafford in *My Time: Making the Most of the Bonus Decades After 50*), the "encore" years (Marc Freedman in *The Big Shift: Navigating the New Stage Beyond Midlife)* or "adulthood II" (Mary Catherine Bateson in *Composing a Further Life: The Age of Active Wisdom)*. Because it's new, this life stage doesn't come with the rites of passage, the social norms or the personal examples that we're used to in making other life transitions. It's going to be up to us to develop those for ourselves and for others who come along behind us.

We're on a frontier. We're blazing a trail. Being on the leading edge can be both exciting and scary ... but to succeed requires that we live smart and think differently about the future. Here's why ...

Midlife Transitions are Different Now

With the prospect of longer life comes two critical questions:

▓ What will I do with these added years?

▓ How will I pay for them?

Most people in our parents' generation knew the answer to those questions — a traditional retirement of leisure was funded with a pension and Social Security. Some people took to it like iron filings to a magnet; others were bored and lonely. But that model became the dream they, and many of us, aspired to.

Except that dream doesn't account for these four factors.

Why Traditional Retirement No Longer Works

1. Traditional retirement doesn't recognize that we're living longer. It doesn't look so bad if it lasts 10 or 15 years. But double that and it starts to look pretty dull and a little like wasting a third of your life.

2. A comfortable retirement is a luxury many cannot afford. Pensions are mostly gone now. They got traded in for 401(k) plans and IRAs, which required us to save for our own retirements. But our retirement savings, if we had the discipline and ability to put money aside, lost value in the economic downturn. Some of us were counting on home equity and that lost value as well. And for anyone who thought Social Security was the answer, it was never intended to fully cover retirement costs.

3. Believe it or not, the workforce will soon shrink, experts say. Generation X, the generation following the boomers, is too small to fill all the jobs that will open as boomers retire. So employers will need to hire or retain older workers to close the gap.

4. Add to this the fact that most of us don't want to fade into insignificance — that we want our lives to continue to count for something, that we want to continue growing and learning, and that we want to make a lasting contribution — and you can see that we live in a world that doesn't favor past models for retirement.

Uncertainty and How to Control It

So what's the result of all this change in our lives? The thing that makes change both exciting and scary is that it breeds UNCERTAINTY.

We're uncertain because we're not sure what to expect, because it's not clear what our options are, because we don't know if others will give us a chance, or because we're tempted to play it safe.

We're also uncertain because we don't know how much money we'll need or how much more we must earn or save. Or we don't know how to generate more income or savings in a slow economy. Or what to do if that isn't possible.

Uncertainty may come in the form of husbands, wives or partners who have different ideas about how to spend these added years. Or from other family members and friends who offer conflicting advice.

It can also come from the tug between working and playing, between helping others and helping ourselves, between making an impact now and creating a legacy for later. Uncertainty upsets balance and balance is one of the things we strive for in our lives.

So what's the antidote for uncertainty? Not surprisingly, it's planning and preparation.

Why Plan and Prepare for the Second Half of Life?

Planning and preparation reduces uncertainty in four ways:

1. **Planning brings things into clearer focus.** It gives us a chance to step back and look at the big picture of our lives. It can shift our understanding of things and open the door to new possibilities we didn't recognize before.

2. **Planning helps us identify and reduce legal, financial and other risks.** This, in turn, eases our anxiety and elevates our confidence about the future.

3. **Preparation expands our choices.** When we plan ahead, we put more options on the table. Waiting for a crisis limits our choices because time for action is short and some options no longer fit our circumstances.

4. **Preparation puts us in a position to "make our own luck."** When pleasant, unexpected surprises come our way—some call it serendipity—we have a framework to determine if the option or the timing is right for us.

Life Planning Defined

Life planning is thinking in a purposeful way about how you want to live. It begins with knowing who you are—your values, strengths and motivations—then applies this knowledge to making choices and setting goals. Life planning helps you take responsibility for and create your best life after 50.

What should you focus on in planning for the second half of your life? That depends on who you are and what your circumstances are. It also depends on what steps you might already have taken to prepare for what comes next in your life.

Life Planning Quiz

Here's a brief quiz — just 10 questions — that will give you an idea about what to focus on and where to start with your life plan. Select the answer that best fits each question.

1. I am clear about my options for continued work beyond midlife, whether for income, to remain active or to use my skills for a useful purpose.

   [Very true] [Somewhat true] [Just getting started] [Not at all]

   (Good Work chapter)

2. I can name ten people (spouse or partner, family, friends, neighbors) I can rely on for intimacy, friendship and support.

   [Very true] [Somewhat true] [Just getting started] [Not at all]

   (The Relationship Dividend chapter)

3. I know what I need to maintain my health, remain active, protect my brain and feel at my best as I grow older.

   [Very true] [Somewhat true] [Just getting started] [Not at all]

   (Well-Being for Life chapter)

4. I have a sense of where, how and with whom I want to live as I age and how to make it happen.

   [Very true] [Somewhat true] [Just getting started] [Not at all]

   (The Right Place chapter)

5. I am clear about my values, how they influence my decisions and what I can do to pass them along to the next generation.

   [Very true] [Somewhat true] [Just getting started] [Not at all]

   (Living in 3D chapter)

6. I know what gives me pleasure, what is fun for me, what to do to relax and how to maintain a sense of balance in my life.

   [Very true] [Somewhat true] [Just getting started] [Not at all]

   (Awaken Your Creativity chapter)

7. I understand what is needed to protect my legal interests while I'm living and to protect the interests of my heirs after I'm gone.

   [Very true] *[Somewhat true]* *[Just getting started]* *[Not at all]*

   (Your Wishes Matter chapter)

8. I have a good idea of how much money I could need for the rest of my life, where it will come from and how to manage it.

   [Very true] *[Somewhat true]* *[Just getting started]* *[Not at all]*

   (Bring Meaning to Money chapter)

9. I know myself well enough to see how my past connects to my future and where to start in determining what comes next in my life.

   [Very true] *[Somewhat true]* *[Just getting started]* *[Not at all]*

   (Your Life Lessons chapter)

10. I have a plan in place that addresses all of the items covered in questions 1-9, and I review and update it regularly.

    [Very true] *[Somewhat true]* *[Just getting started]* *[Not at all]*

Review your answers as a guide to how to read this book, beginning with the chapters that relate to the questions you answered "Not at all," followed by the chapters responding to your "Just getting started" answers, etc. Remember, to live smart may require you to begin with areas that are less familiar, or more difficult for you to engage with.

Developing a Roadmap for Your Life

So, you might be saying to yourself, "This sounds like a big job. How does it work for someone like me?" Okay, we don't promise that creating a roadmap for your life will be easy, but three things will help guide you, and help you to live smart in this new stage of life.

1. A checklist will help make sure you don't leave anything out.

2. A process will help you measure your progress and see next steps.

3. A source of support, often from a coach or adviser, will help you avoid mistakes, get unstuck, see possibilities and find resources.

Let's take a look at each one.

1. The Checklist

As the quiz suggests, there are many parts of our lives. These are all interrelated but we tend to view them separately because the professionals we see are specialists in one part or another. We wouldn't ask our doctor about taxes or our yoga instructor about insurance. But since a decision in one part of life can affect others, we need to consider them all, either together or in turn.

The various aspects of life are like the facets of a gemstone — each offers a different perspective on your life. Like a room with many doors, they let you view your life from different angles.

We've developed the following checklist that identifies eight aspects of life. It shows what each aspect covers and some of the questions that arise at this new stage of life. Use this list to identify the aspects that are of highest concern to you. You can also use it to keep track of what you're working on and note your progress.

Checklist for Life Planning

Aspects	Covers	Questions	Priority	Done
Work	Contribution, meaning, purpose	What to do? Who to be?		
Love	Intimacy, family, friends	Who to love? How to connect?		
Health	Lifestyle, energy, brain	How to stay well and keep active?		
Home	Place, belonging, safety	Where to live? With whom to live?		

Aspects	Covers	Questions	Priority	Done
Legacy	Values, impact, wisdom	What to give? How to help others?		
Leisure	Play, learning, creativity	How to have fun, achieve balance?		
Legal	Control, risk management	How to anticipate and prepare?		
Money	Security, responsibility	What to earn, save and spend?		

2. The Process

People go through predictable steps in a life planning process. Sometimes the steps are labeled and set up differently, but they all share a common purpose and direction.

Steps in the Life Planning Process

1. **Assess who you are now:** What are your motivations, values, interests and skills?

2. **Discover possibilities:** What are your options and opportunities?

3. **Clarify goals:** What do you want to achieve? Who do you want to become?

4. **Make changes:** What is your plan? What do you need? Who can help?

5. **Adjust as needed:** How do you stay aligned? How do you manage change?

As you can see, these steps move forward from one to the next. But you'll probably find that you need to double back at times to deal with things you didn't expect. This cyclical approach might be needed if something changes that you didn't anticipate, like a family health issue, a new opportunity or ... winning the lottery!

Even with planned changes, like a relocation to be near grandkids or leaving a paying position, cycling back through these steps will support the decisions and actions needed to manage the transition.

3. Source of Support

Many of us tend to approach a process like this by trial and error, if we make any effort at all. The problem is that trial and error often takes a long time. And often the trials are frustrating and errors add up to disappointment.

The alternative is to seek out resources that are designed to help you get results. There are several possibilities you might consider:

- Work with a life planner, life coach, counselor or adviser who has experience assisting people with second-half-of-life transitions.

- Work with a financial life planner (a financial planner or adviser who has additional training to assist you with non-financial life planning issues).

- Work with a community-based organization that provides transition services geared for people over age 50.

- Work with someone in another specialty (housing, wellness, law, etc.) who has a professional relationship that allows you to connect to one of the above.

- Work on your own with the aid of instructional books, websites or workbooks with support from a trusted friend or family member.

You can find sources of support like these by checking the directory and resources pages of the Life Planning Network website, www.lifeplanningnetwork.org.

Working with a Life Planning Professional

It's best to work with an adviser, coach or counselor who knows something about each of the aspects of life shown in the Checklist for Life Planning and who can help you integrate these into a coherent plan. Life planning professionals often have relationships with or can refer you to other professionals when needed. That way you get assistance that adds to your life planning professional's offerings.

If you decide to work with a life planning professional, keep in mind that some life planning approaches are highly structured and others are open-ended. Some involve face-to-face meetings and others happen by telephone or email. Some occur one-on-one and others involve working in groups.

The options are many so it's important to know what will work best for you. Do you need someone to help you think through your interests and personal preferences, introduce you to resources, guide you through a process, or connect you to the experiences of others who have made similar transitions?

Is your personal style to work one-on-one, with a group or on your own? Do you feel an urgency to move quickly or will you take whatever time is required to allow events to unfold at their own pace? Does your best thinking come from bouncing ideas off others, writing in a journal, sitting in quiet contemplation or listening to others tell their stories?

Understanding your own preferences and financial resources is the first step in selecting the right professional partner or approach for beginning the life planning process. Another step is to understand the background, experience and style of the person or persons you will be working with. How long have they been doing this work and what have been the outcomes? Ask for references.

Also be sure to understand how fees work, how referrals will be made to other professionals if needed, what steps are recommended, and how you will measure progress in your work together.

If you choose to participate in a transition support group or work on your own, be sure to use tools and resources that deal with the full range of topics covered by the Checklist.

Managing Transition

By the time we reach midlife, most of us have had a good deal of experience with transition. We can use this experience to help us manage the transitions that lie ahead. Though we may not know the specifics, we've learned what to expect and that, in time, we'll make it through.

Some transitions can be easy and others more challenging. Sometimes they require that we give something up. Even though we may be gaining something of value in its place, the experience of change can cause sadness, frustration, even anger. We can also experience change as relief, adventure or exhilaration.

Whatever the emotions (and they may be mixed), transition is a process that evolves. William Bridges, in his book *Transitions: Making Sense of Life's Changes*, suggests three phases of transition that we go through.

First comes a period of *letting go*. This is followed by a *neutral zone*, a period during which we may feel muddled, puzzled and confused. But gradually we come to see things more clearly. After letting go of our old identity, our perspective shifts and new ideas come into view. The final stage is called a *new beginning*. This is where the transition process leads to a new stability and life goes on in a more predictable way.

Another helpful way to think about transition comes from Richard Leider and David Shapiro in their book *Repacking Your Bags: Lighten Your Load for the Rest of Your Life*. They say we carry a lot of excess baggage into midlife and recommend that we pause to lay it all out, select what's needed for the journey forward, and let go of the rest.

Then we can repack our bags, taking only what's of value for the next phase of life. This metaphor is another way to think about the life planning process. We pause, take stock, then find (or build) a new way forward.

How to Use This Book

LIVE SMART AFTER 50! discusses issues and options that apply to a new life stage that begins in the 50s or 60s and often continues into the 80s and beyond. The contributors to this book look at these issues and options from the view of individuals like you as well as the communities and society in which we all live.

This is not intended as a comprehensive guide or a how-to book. Instead, we hope it gives you a good understanding of how to navigate the transitions and plan for a meaningful, purposeful and satisfying second half of your life.

Each chapter looks at key topics related to the facets of life after 50. Checklists and other exercises give you a way to think about these topics and discuss them with your spouse or partner, your family and friends, and your life planning professional(s).

Resources offered in the text or at the end of each chapter provide additional information on specific topics. Out of the flood of books, articles and websites available on these subjects, we believe these resources are the most helpful.

Feel free to skip around the book as your interest leads you. It's designed to make sense if read this way as much as reading it from cover to cover. However you approach the book, remember that all of these topics are interrelated and interconnected—they don't stand alone.

We recommend sharing this book with your spouse or partner and with close friends. Anyone who has a stake in your plans will want to know what you're thinking. This book is a good way to open the door to those conversations.

This book may also be helpful to friends, colleagues, neighbors and others who face their own midlife transitions. Even if the topic hasn't come up, they may be silently wrestling with questions about what's next in their own lives. They will thank you for introducing them to a source that can help.

Finally, share this book with your life planning professional or with other professionals whose advice touches on any of the categories covered here. This will broaden the context of your relationship with them and enable you to take the first step toward a life plan that integrates and balances all of the relevant parts.

We hope you look back on this as the starting point for a purposeful, satisfying new stage of life, one filled with meaning, opportunity, contentment and fun. Enjoy the journey!

About the Life Planning Network

This book was written by members of the Life Planning Network, a community of professionals dedicated to helping people navigate the second half of life. We represent a variety of planning disciplines ranging from career counselors and financial advisers to life coaches, health and fitness professionals, and estate lawyers.

What brings us together is a belief that people need to carefully and intentionally plan for this new stage of life. And they need to do it in a way that connects all the dots of their lives.

We wrote this book for two reasons. First, we want to spread the word. Because this life stage is new and doesn't have a name yet, many people aren't aware of it. If they're not aware of it, they can't take the steps needed to make the most of it.

And that leads to the second reason. We want everyone to think constructively about what they do with these "bonus" / "encore" years. In doing so, we hope they will see the possibilities, better manage the uncertainties and take advantage of the opportunities.

We believe people can and should continue to be contributing members of society in the second half of their lives. We think they should be recognized and valued for the benefit of their accumulated experience and wisdom. They should be seen as assets, not liabilities.

The authors of this book are experts in their respective fields. They have contributed to the book as a public service to readers and out of support for the mission of the Life Planning Network. Please visit our website to access our directory of members, including the authors, or to learn more about the Life Planning Network, www.lifeplanningnetwork.org

Life Planning Network Chapter Contributor

Doug Dickson, President, Discovering What's Next, *www.discoveringwhatsnext.com.*

Resources

Our Changing World

Frederick R. Lynch, *One Nation Under AARP: The Fight Over Medicare, Social Security, and America's Future*, University of California Press, 2011.

Abigail Trafford, *My Time: Making the Most of the Bonus Decades After 50*, Basic Books, 2004.

Marc Freedman, *The Big Shift: Navigating the New Stage Beyond Midlife*, Public Affairs, 2011.

Mary Catherine Bateson, *Composing a Further Life: The Age of Active Wisdom*, Random House Digital, 2010.

Transition

William Bridges, *Transitions: Making Sense of Life's Changes*, Perseus Books Publishing, 1980.

Richard J. Leider and David A. Shapiro, *Repacking Your Bags: Lighten Your Load for the Rest of Your Life*, ReadHowYouWant, 2008.

Directory of Life Planning Professionals

www.lifeplanningnetwork.org, website of the Life Planning Network, including a directory of life planning professionals.

Your Life Lessons —
Building the future on your past

WE HAVE A THEORY in life planning — that when we take the time to make sense of what we have experienced in our lives so far, we can make much wiser plans for our future.

Enhancing or increasing awareness of ourselves can be a valuable first step in the life planning process. So many of us merely react to life ... a situation arises and we respond. The more knowledge we have about ourselves, the more we can be proactive and therefore more in control of our life course.

We become more self-aware and understand ourselves better by reflecting on what we do and why we do it. From the foundation of this reflection, we can consider how we might do things differently to achieve greater success. Becoming aware of our own emotions, and how they influence our behaviors, helps us learn to channel them in order to achieve what we want from life.

What's Your Life Story Telling You?

After 50-plus years, many of us have stories to tell ... of achievements, losses, relationships and careers. Think of those experiences like ingredients in a recipe. They can each stand on their own, but when combined, they produce something different and unique ... our life story. Discovering your life story can be a powerful way to begin the second half of life's journey.

Up until age 50, most of us have been on the roller coaster of life — education, dating, marriage, career and parenting — with little time to step off and reflect on where we've been.

It's at this stage of our lives, after the kids are grown or we're established in our careers, that we have a moment to be introspective. During this time the process of discovering more about ourselves can take on greater importance.

As empty nesters, we may ask, "If I'm not Mom or Dad, who am I?"

If we're unhappy in our job, we may raise the question, "If I'm not (*insert job title here*), what am I?"

And some of us feel restless and begin to think, "Who do I *want* to be?"

Many of us don't know what to do when these questions come up. We can gain deeper insight into who we are and what we want out of life by starting with our past. Our experiences tell a story about how we adapt to challenges and opportunities. Our story highlights our strengths and our vulnerabilities. By creating an integrated view of our life, we have a powerful tool to understand how we might approach the future.

Everybody has a life story. It's too bad most people don't know theirs.

The memories and experiences that have shaped your life are unique to you; no two stories are the same. One of the many benefits of creating a life story is that you learn more about your uniqueness, what *you* believe, what matters most to you, and what the sum of your life experiences has taught you.

The Lifeline Exercise

The Lifeline Exercise is a simple method to help interpret how key events have shaped your life, and a good predictor of how you might act in the future. Take a look at the Lifeline Exercise (Appendix A), and be sure to set aside about 30 minutes of quiet time to go through it.

Angela reviewed her lifeline. At age 54, she'd had a number of challenges in life—a childhood illness that left her disfigured, the death of her boyfriend at age 19 and more surgery in her 20s that left her unable to have children. She'd had a number of high points, too—scholastic success, a happy marriage and a good career with many promotions. She was a recognized leader at work and in her community.

An "aha" came to her as she reviewed her life story. Angela's early setbacks had strengthened her will and determination to overcome life's challenges at a very early age. It became clear to Angela that she applied that same determination to other life experiences like her schoolwork and business life, and that had helped to make her successful.

Angela's happiest times came when she helped others. High up on her lifeline were two notable experiences: one leading a mentoring program at work and the other volunteering at a children's ward in her local hospital. Angela also felt personal success when she led work teams to reach their goals, especially when she took a small department and grew it into one of the most profitable departments in her company. Recently, Angela has been considering a career transition to lead a nonprofit for children with disabilities. Now she could see why this calling was so strong, and how it fit as the next chapter in her life story.

We hope you will take the time to create your lifeline. Like Angela, it may give you insight into where you've been and what's next.

Your lifeline is also powerful when shared. You may have important life lessons that you might like to share with your loved ones. Your stories can be a gift of love and a cherished legacy to your children or grandchildren.

Living Your Values

Roger Federer values achievement. Donald Trump values power. How do we know this? Values are a person's driving force that influences their actions and reactions. Federer would not have won major tennis titles if achievement was not an important value of his. "The Donald" would not have created a TV show where he gets to point his finger to a host of celebrities and say "You're Fired!" if power were not one of his significant values.

Where else do our values come from? We inherit some of our values. For example, often times our sense of right and wrong come from the values our parents hold. We learn some values from our teachers and other influential people in our lives. We also take on values from reading and watching TV and from our various experiences. Our values can reflect the values of the place we live, the town, region or country.

Values are also generational. The social upheaval during the 1960s caused many baby boomers to question the relevance of institutions, morals and intellectual conclusions of the times. As a result, core generational values for boomers revolve around their focus on self and individuality. In his book, *Baby Boomer Blues*, author Gary Collins identifies other common boomer values including: relevance, questioning, instant remedies, participation, acceptance, informality, flexibility, lack of commitment, and enthusiasm for causes. He also believes boomers have high expectations, value autonomy, and they are non-traditional, driven and nostalgic.

Why is it important to know what our values are? So we can make *better choices*. When we know what our personal values are, our decision-making becomes infinitely easier. Knowing how to make decisions that satisfy your own important values, and not those of others, means that our sense of self is strengthened by every decision.

For example Paul, a writer, highly values independence — being free from the influence, guidance and control of others. Knowing this, and in order to stay true to his values, Paul searches for work projects that allow him his independence in order to flourish.

Our values determine our decisions and guide our lives. Once we identify values that are meaningful to us, we can also understand how our values drive our behavior. We demonstrate our values in action in our personal behavior, work behavior, decision making, contributions and interpersonal behavior.

People who don't know their values or don't live by their values can be influenced in ways that take them off course. Knowing your values helps you in decision making because it gives you a moral compass that offers a clear set of rules that allow you to quickly know what good choices are for you and what are not. Knowing your values helps you to find compatible people, places and things that support you and provide you comfort. And knowing your values can help you to live with integrity, being true to yourself.

We're in our second half of life, so why haven't we discovered our values by now?

For some of us, we just haven't taken the time to examine what motivates us. And sometimes we have conflicting values, someone gets ill, we lose our job, our children's needs come first, we have money problems and job changes and we do things to survive and get by. These situations may cause us to act in ways that don't align with our values.

Cathy's #1 value is fun. (Yes, fun is a real value!) Cathy enjoys playing games and getting together with friends at her home. Cathy also values family. When Cathy's father died, Cathy moved her mom, Sophie, close to her in an assisted living facility. She visited her mom weekly and took her to the movies, to church and out to dinner. But now at age 96, Sophie's health has declined. Cathy is visiting her mom daily and sometimes multiple times a day to give her meds, take her to doctor appointments and to perform a host of other caregiving duties. Between her full time job and her mom, Cathy has no time for fun. She is depressed and stressed. Her values are in conflict.

Values can be confusing too because they are often subjective; they mean different things to different people. The value of achievement may mean multiple Grand Slam wins to Roger Federer and it may mean a successful real estate empire to Donald Trump.

You can determine your values in a few ways — here are two that we like …

Life Values Self-Assessment Test

The first is an online tool created by the midlife career website WhatsNext.com. The **Life Values Self-Assessment Test** (LVAT) works by asking you to compare 11 life values to each other and to indicate which of the two is more important to work on in order for you to achieve a satisfying and well-balanced life. The LVAT uses your answers to rank order the relative importance of each value based on your responses. This test is somewhat limited, in that it has only 11 pre-selected life values, but it can be a good first start at understanding what values are important to you at this time. Check out the Life Values Self-Assessment Test and start comparing.

Personal Mission Statement Builder

The second tool is authored by the time management and assessment firm Franklin Covey. The **Franklin Covey Personal Mission Statement Builder** provides a view of your key values as a result of creating your personal mission statement. The online tool guides you through a series of questions. As you read your completed mission statement, you'll become aware of the personal values that guide you to answer the questions in a particular way. Since our goals and our life purpose are grounded in our values, this exercise takes identifying our key values to the next level. Take a look and build your own personal mission statement.

Living your values is one of the most powerful tools available to you to help you be the person you want to be, help you accomplish your goals and dreams, and leave a positive legacy.

Discovering Your Strengths

Strengths are character traits that all of us have. Unlike talents which are inborn, we can develop and grow our strengths. Using our strengths makes us feel good because they express our true values. Our strengths are some of our best tools for accomplishing our goals and leading a satisfying life.

Each of us has strengths that are key to who we are. These are called our *signature strengths*. Oftentimes we become aware of our strengths through other people's observations. Dori's parents point out her natural humor, Curt's boss comments on his leadership skills in his performance review and Meg's friends remark on her kindness and generosity to others. Identifying our strengths beyond what's pointed out to us can provide further insight into ourselves.

VIA Survey of Character Strengths

A number of tools can help you discover your strengths. One we like best is the **VIA Survey of Character Strengths,** located on the Authentic Happiness Research site. The survey can be accessed online free. After you answer a 240-question survey, your top five strengths are identified. You'll be given an ordered list of your 24 strengths. The top five are your Signature Strengths. Take the VIA Survey of Character Strengths and start learning about your strengths. For more information on your list, we recommend the book *Authentic Happiness* by Martin E.P. Seligman.

Once you have identified your top strengths, ask yourself these questions:

- Do your signature strengths match up with those you use in your work? If not, can you adjust your job so that they do?

- How do your strengths fit with your partner or spouse?

- Which strengths give you the most energy when you use them? How can you use them more?

- How do your strengths contribute to your interests and passions? Can you develop other interests based on your strengths?

Pay particular attention to your top five strengths. These can be used when you're stuck with a problem. Ask yourself, how can I use my strength of _____ to solve this dilemma? By finding new ways to use your signature strengths regularly, you become more authentically you and feel good at the same time.

Knowing How You're Wired

Our **intrinsic motivation** guides our behaviors and choices. For example, the food we eat (organic vs. fast), the investment choices we make (stocks vs. bonds), the social activities we pursue (gardening vs. competing in triathlons) and whether we willingly plan for a bright future.

Intrinsic motivation refers to motivation that's driven by our interest or enjoyment in the task itself. It exists within us without any external pressure.

Understanding your intrinsic motivation and how to use it to pursue or reframe your goals provides a sense of self-awareness that can lead to positive personal change.

One model for understanding intrinsic motivation suggests each of us can be categorized as a "hopes and aspirations" person or a "duties and obligations" person.*

Individuals who have a "hopes and aspirations" mindset are more likely to actively pursue goals and engage in behaviors *to achieve desired states*. An example of this might be losing weight to look great for your upcoming high school reunion.

Individuals who have a "duties and obligations" mindset actively engage to *avoid undesired end-states*. An example of this might be losing weight to avoid another year of the doctor admonishing you on your annual visit.

An interesting consequence of such motivation orientations is that it guides so many of our day-to-day behaviors and often affects the first thoughts we have about a given activity.

Peter, a CPA with a masters in taxation, is a "duties and obligations" person. As a professional, he was drawn to work that avoids

---

* For more on regulatory focus theory see Grewal et al. (2010), "Understanding How to Achieve Competitive Advantage through Regulatory Fit: A Meta-Analysis," Marketing Science Institute Reports. *Working Paper Series 2010, Report No 10-117* and Higgins, E. Tory (2002), "How Self-Regulation Creates Distinct Values: The Case of Promotion and Prevention Decision-Making," *Journal of Consumer Psychology*, 12 (3), 177-91.

the negative effects of high taxes for his company. Peter methodically analyzes most situations before making a decision, with the goal of averting any negative consequences of a bad choice. With regard to financial life planning, Peter may more easily achieve his goal when he frames it as averting the possibility of outliving his money vs. having enough money to enjoy in his days of leisure.

In contrast, Lori, a 50-plus fitness coach is a "hopes and aspirations" individual. Lori was drawn to her profession because it's a good fit with her intrinsic motivation. Daily, she helps her clients focus on the positive benefits of exercise — losing weight, feeling better, having more energy and a greater sense of self-esteem.

Many of us have a blend of "hopes and aspirations" and "duties and obligations" motivations. On reflection, which one do you find most dominant in your life? Developing an understanding of our own mental motivations can help us to frame (or reframe) our goals so that we have a better chance of accomplishing them.

All of This Adds Up to Self-Awareness

Self-awareness allows us to explore our individual personalities, value systems, beliefs, natural inclinations and tendencies. Because we are all different in the way we react to things, learn and synthesize information, it's helpful at this stage of our lives to spend some time in self-reflection to gain a better insight into ourselves and to understand others, especially the people we live and work with.

Our life story, our values, our strengths and our intrinsic motivation all contribute to our self-awareness. Self-awareness is not an endpoint, but rather a process. This process begins and ends with life itself. We are constantly taking in information about the world around us, and experiencing the world within us.

It takes some reflection time, however, to gain understanding and self-awareness from the experiences and information we have. When we take the time to make sense of what we've experienced in our lives so far, we can make much wiser plans for our future.

We hope you take the time to reflect on your life in whatever way is best for you. The tools suggested in this chapter provide a place to begin. In the chapters that follow, other tools and questions will prompt further exploration into your values and intrinsic motivations as they apply to other areas in your life. The more you understand about yourself, the more effective your goals and action plans will be for smart living in the uncertain times ahead.

Life Planning Network Chapter Contributors

Andrea Gallagher, Certified Senior Advisor, President Senior Concerns, 2011-2012 President of Life Planning Network (LPN). www.seniorconcerns.org. (Chapter Leader)

Natalie Eldridge, PhD, Psychologist and Life Transition Coach, Author of *Action on Purpose* Newsletter, www.EldridgeWorks.com.

Kit Harrington Hayes, MEd, Founder and Principal of LifeWork Design, Author of *Managing Career Transitions*, www.KitHayes.com.

Meg Newhouse, PhD, CPCC, Certified Life Coach, Author of *Life Planning for the Third Age*, www.passionandpurpose.com.

Candy Spitz, LCSW, ACC, Career and Life Coach, www.boomerslifecoach.com.

Resources

Marcus Buckingham and Donald O. Clifton, *Now, Discover Your Strengths*, The Free Press, 2001.

Gary R. Collins and Timothy E. Clinton, *Baby Boomer Blues*, W Publishing Group, 1992.

The Dalai Lama and Howard C. Cutler, *The Art of Happiness: A Handbook for Living*, Riverhead Books, 1998.

Anthony de Mello, *Awareness: The Perils and Opportunity of Reality*, Doubleday, 1990.

Pamila D. McLean and Frederic M. Hudson, *Life Launch: A Passionate Guide to the Rest of Your Life*, 5th Edition, Hudson Institute, 2011.

Martin E.P. Seligman, *Authentic Happiness*, Free Press by Simon & Schuster, 2002.

Judith Viorst, *Necessary Losses: The Loves, Illusions, Dependencies and Impossible Expectations That All of Us Have to Give up in Order to Grow Older*, Fawcett Gold Medal, 1986.

Franklin Covey Mission Statement Builder at www.franklincovey.com/msb/

VIA Survey of Character Strengths at www.authentichappiness.sas.upenn.edu/

What's Next Life Values Assessment Test at www.whatsnext.com

The Relationship Dividend—
Thriving through connection and community

> *"How does one keep from 'growing old inside'? Surely only in community! The only way to make friends with time is to stay friends with people."*
> — *Robert McAfee Brown*

HAVING HEALTHY RELATIONSHIPS AND a supportive community is one of the most important predictors of health and happiness as we age. And there's no better time than NOW to start making choices that will increase your sense of well-being today and in the future. Whether you're single or partnered, having adequate resources and a supportive network is crucial. If you're isolated or don't have the support in place, it's time to find or create a community based on your needs, values and interests.

According to the Relationship Institute at UCLA, "Relationships equal health, wealth and happiness. People who are in good relationships have better mental and physical health. They don't become sick as often, and recover more quickly from illness."

What's different about second half of life relationships?

Have you ever felt like time was flying by and all of a sudden you're thinking about retirement, Social Security and Medicare? As we get older it often feels that time passes more quickly. Aging changes our perspective and with it the awareness that life does not go on forever.

In midlife, we may begin to think more seriously about what's really important in life and in relationships.

During the first half of life our roles and responsibilities are related to learning, building careers and raising families. By midlife, we have outlived many of the old roles and taken on new ones. Whether it's becoming a grandparent or caring for elderly parents, we need to be able to adapt to the changes that life brings.

Some Things to Think About

▩ **How are your relationships different now?**

▩ **How do you think your roles could change in the future?**

▩ **How will the life changes you anticipate impact or be supported by your relationships?**

As values shift from success and materialism to meaning and purpose, the *quality* of relationships becomes more important in the second half of life. What we once needed and wanted from others may be very different from our current needs and desires. We may seek out deeper, more authentic relationships to satisfy our changing needs.

Compared to previous generations, we have a great deal of *choice* in how we lead our lives. Thanks to the birth control pill, higher education of women, and the increasing acceptability of alternative lifestyles (lesbian, gay, bisexual, transgender, etc.), the percentage of baby boomers with *no living children* is almost twice what it was in previous generations.

Aging without grown children, grandchildren or other close family members raises a host of questions, such as, who will be there to help me when I need it? Who will make decisions on my behalf when I'm no longer able to? Who will carry on my legacy? If this is your situation, it's important to think ahead, get whatever information you need and plan for the future.

There is no denying that illness and loss become more prevalent in the second half of life. Maybe you've already experienced the loss of important relationships through life changes—retirement, job loss, moves or the death of loved ones. Finding ways to get support and connect with others can be healing and is important for your general health and well-being.

Some changes brew for years and others come unexpectedly. With the increase in longevity over the past several years, there has been a growing trend toward divorce in long-term marriages with one or both partners seeking a more satisfying life with a new partner or on their own.

> *A 2011 U.S. Census report found that over time, despite increasing life expectancies, fewer first-time married couples were making it to their 25th, 30th, and 35th wedding anniversaries.*
>
> *—Kelly Greene*

While it can be wonderful to have a compatible life partner, not everyone does. But many other relationships exist in life and connection is the best prescription for healthy aging.

- **What are you noticing about your relationships?**

- **How can you meet people with similar interests and values?**

- **What can you do to deepen or enhance the relationships you have?**

The second half of life is an opportunity to decide what's really important and where, how and with whom you want to spend your precious time. It's a time to clarify your needs and consider what you have to share and give back to your community.

Whom Do You Want in YOUR Life?

As you move into the next phase of life, it may be helpful to think about the people around you. Who are they? How did your relationship develop? What do you have in common?

In addition to family, the majority of people in our lives tend to be old friends, work colleagues, people with similar interests, neighbors, those we met when our children were young and others from our religious or spiritual communities. Some of these friendships may deepen over time. Others may slip away as our interests and our lives change.

The diagram below shows the different groups of relationships you might have.

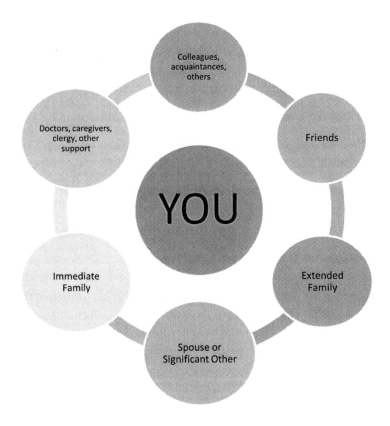

Think about your own relationships. How do they fit into this diagram? Let's look briefly at some of the circles.

Spouse or Significant Other

A spouse or significant other is, for many people, their primary and most enduring relationship. Not only do they need to survive the many ups and downs of life, couples also need to be able to cope with change — change in health, appearance, lifestyles, needs and priorities. People who work with couples find that patience, commitment, caring and the ability for honest, open communication are necessary for partners to be able to plan together for the future. Relationships also require periodic revitalization and renewal.

How are you doing in revitalizing and renewing your most important relationship?

Family — Immediate and Extended

Your immediate family generally includes your children (whether or not they are living at home) and grandchildren. Your relationship with your children has probably changed over the years and will continue to change as time goes by. Maintaining healthy family relationships is important. We'll talk more about "healthy" relationships later in this chapter.

- How close are you today with your children?

- What parts of the relationships are satisfying? What parts are not?

- What are the unresolved issues you have with one or more of your children?

Your extended family includes all the people who share your ancestry or lineage that are not part of your immediate family. Prior to the middle of the twentieth century, most extended families stayed close to one another and helped each other, often on a farm or in a family business. This began to change in the latter 1900s. Some of you might have experienced this closeness when you were a child.

All families, just like their members, have personalities. You could probably describe your family in quite colorful terms! Some families are large; some are small. Some families are close-knit and see each other often; others are more distant either geographically or emotionally. Some families are warm and open; others are closed and more insular.

How would you describe your family?

Unless you have a family member who is abusive or unavailable, it's generally worth the time and energy it takes to stay connected. This is especially true of your immediate family. As we age, family relationships often become more important. The second half of life can be a time for resolving past issues and deepening relationships. *Who matters to you?*

Friends

> *"Friends are the family we choose for ourselves."*
> —Edna Buchanan

There is nothing quite like having a friend who has known you for years, and witnessed your life events and transitions. They know the good, the bad and the ugly, and love you anyway. Nurturing your friendships will most likely be an important component to your second half of life. The conversations will change over time as life issues change. Where you once shared stories and challenges about work, child rearing or romantic entanglements, you may now find concerns focus on health issues, caregiving or whether to downsize your home. And the conversation isn't all that's bound to change as you age. You may be involved in taking care of a sick friend or helping them out with a family crisis. In the second half of life, "in sickness or in health" is not just for spouses!

Many people in midlife have already lost friends. People move away, their interests and needs change and sadly, some die. Or it may be time to say goodbye to a relationship that drains your time and energy.

Life transitions such as leaving a job, moving to a new community or separating from a spouse or partner can also mean the loss of close relationships. But transitions can also be an opportunity to bring new relationships into your life.

Take a minute to think about the people you would include in the "friends" circle in the diagram. Which are old friendships? Which are new friendships? How have these relationships changed?

Women tend to connect and make friends more easily than men. It's not a bias, it's a fact. Men may have work colleagues or sports buddies but often don't continue these relationships over time. Of course, none of this is universal, so if you're looking to meet new friends begin with what interests you:

▓ Find and join an interest group (e.g. gardening, quilting, woodworking, model building)

▓ Take an adult education class (e.g. photography, ceramics, drawing, ancient history)

▓ Focus on a sport (e.g. take golf lessons, join a tennis ladder, sign up for a biking tour)

▓ Get involved in a cause you care about (e.g. volunteer at an animal shelter, join an election campaign team, serve on a non-profit board)

▓ Join a game group (e.g. bridge, mahjong, Scrabble®)

▓ Sign up for group travel — as a couple or with a singles group

▓ Take a full- or part-time job — something you're interested in and where you can learn new skills and meet new people.

(Teach at a nearby college, community adult education, or senior center; walk dogs for your working neighbors; be a census data collector; hire yourself out on contract to _____ (fill in the blank with what you know)_____.)

As long as you can find a way to get out and participate in something you enjoy, you'll find people who share some of your interests and passions. Don't be a recluse. It very often leads to loneliness and depression — something we all want to avoid.

Colleagues, Acquaintances, Doctors, Clergy, Caregivers and Other Professionals

In addition, you may have a whole host of other people who don't fit into the above categories. These are people who come into our lives out of need or circumstances. Some of these relationships may last for years. It's not uncommon to have a trusted physician that has known you for several years and taken care of every ache and pain you've ever experienced. Other relationships may naturally fall away as circumstances change. You may be close to colleagues at work but job changes often mean relationships change even with the best intention of keeping in touch. In our busy lives, maintaining relationships takes energy and effort. The relationships that endure over time are probably those that are most important to you.

What are Supportive and Healthy Relationships?

We have put together a worksheet of 10 specific characteristics that we believe are common to all supportive, healthy relationships. These characteristics apply to any relationship, not just your spouse or significant other and not *every* relationship has *all* of these characteristics. Take a look at the *Relationship Assessment Worksheet* and accompanying questions in Appendix B — they can provide you with a gauge to develop and deepen the important relationships in your life.

Having a good relationship takes the commitment of two people who are invested in each other and willing to put in time, energy and attention for the sake of the relationship. The opportunity to create this with another person is rewarding and satisfying. What could be better than having mutual trust and caring with the important people in your life? And the basis of healthy, satisfying relationships is being able to communicate effectively and problem solve together.

Tips for good communication:

▓ Set aside a time and space to talk without distractions

▓ Listen to each other without interrupting

▓ Don't make assumptions

▓ Don't blame each other

▓ Remember that sometimes you need to agree to disagree

Gain or Drain and Knowing when it's Time to "Let Go"

All too often, we're so busy taking care of others that we forget about our own needs or fail to clearly express them. This can occur in relationships with our partners as well as with other people in our lives. Asserting our own needs can sometimes be difficult.

Have you ever been in a relationship where you were consistently giving more than you were receiving?

If so, you know how draining this can be. Consider the following example:

Sue was a good listener and always offered a shoulder to cry on. When her husband died, she had no one to turn to and decided to get together with Mary who was also a widow. But Mary soon began calling Sue three or more evenings a week, complaining about her loneliness. Sue felt that the friendship was "one-sided" and started dreading Mary's calls.

Sue was emotionally and physically drained. At this time in her life, she didn't want to prolong a relationship in which she wasn't getting her needs met. But she liked Mary and decided to share how she was feeling. Sue took a risk that paid off. She and Mary were able to talk more openly about what they both needed and renegotiated how they would spend time together. Meeting weekly for coffee and mutual support seemed a good compromise and the evening phone calls stopped.

You may be thinking, what about my needs? Are they being met? Is there a "Mary" in my life? A word of caution! Please don't come to the conclusion that if a relationship is less than perfect you have to get rid of it. We all have issues with partners, friends, relatives and others. As with Mary and Sue, given a chance, change is often possible when people are willing to accept responsibility for their behavior and put effort into resolving what isn't working in a relationship. But there are times that relationships are irreparable and saying goodbye can free both of you to move on in your lives.

Setting a Personal Boundary

- Reflect on how you're feeling and what you need.

- Decide what boundary (often words or actions) you need to set to take care of yourself.

- When and how will you do this?

- How will you decide if it's time to "let go" of the friendship or relationship?

It Takes a Village —
Living and Aging in Community

As Secretary of State Hillary Rodham Clinton once said, "It takes a village to raise a child." To paraphrase, it takes a village, or community, to support us as we journey through life, and even more so as we age. Community often refers to people with common social norms and values who live in the same geographic location. But this is just one form of community. Community is also a social, virtual or family network. It can be school or work-based, faith or spiritually based, or health related. Communities generally offer a sense of togetherness and belonging as well as a division of work and cooperation. Finding or developing a nurturing and sustaining community takes effort and commitment.

Jan and Tom, both in their early sixties, were semi-retired "empty nesters" dealing with life transitions, relationships and making choices about "what's next." Some of their challenges might sound familiar. Jan and Tom decided to move to the city after living in the suburbs for many years. They were optimistic and excited but didn't anticipate how challenging it would be to leave the security and familiarity of their long-time community. They quickly discovered that it was more difficult in later life to feel like they "belonged" in a new environment. They began to explore interests and activities to connect with people, make friends and create a sense of community in their new environment.

How Communities Develop

Communities can develop around shared values, stage of life, goals, interests or causes. Jan and Tom might have looked for a community of people who were also dealing with issues related to midlife change and transition. Senior and intergenerational communities have been developed by people who couldn't find what they needed and decided to create it. Some people prefer being in communities with people of similar ages and values and others prefer more diversity in a multicultural and intergenerational community. There's no "right way," only what's right for you.

Communities can be helpful to professionals as well. The Life Planning Network, the organization responsible for this book, is a national community for interdisciplinary professionals who share common values and goals. Members around the country meet periodically in person and virtually, learning from and supporting each other.

Most communities offer services and programs through senior councils on aging, senior centers, and through churches or temples. Programs such as lecture series, cultural events, exercise classes, virtual interest-based groups that meet on the Internet and other resources that support healthy aging are usually open to the general public and bring people together — a necessary ingredient for building community.

Where Do You Belong?

Finding the right community might happen naturally or it may take effort and introspection. Living near children or grandchildren may be your priority with other things being secondary. Or you may need to stay close to aging parents. Your focus may be on a faith-based or spiritual community. Finding where you belong is a complicated process based on your values, interests, needs and desires. And those may change over time.

Before making a major decision like moving or choosing a different lifestyle, think ahead about how and where you will fit into this new setting. It can ultimately make the difference between success and disappointment. You can learn more about finding the right community in the chapter titled "The Right Place," and by using the *Clarifying Housing and Community Preferences Checklist* in Appendix C to help you plan wisely.

An often forgotten aspect of finding the right community is how you meet and connect with people. Some of us are more outgoing and others more introverted. Knowing your own style of connecting will help you decide how willing you are to step out of your comfort zone to build community or whether you want a ready-made community. What's important is having a community of caring, like-minded people whom you can connect with in the second half of life.

When you consider joining or building a community, you face many choices. Making good decisions will involve answering the questions WHERE, WHEN, WHO and WHY. The *Clarifying Housing and Community Preferences Checklist* can help you think about what kind of community you'd like to live in.

As you can see, there are many factors to consider as you think about creating your community and it may not be possible to have *everything* you want in one place. You may need to ask yourself, "What's most important to me at this time in my life?" Prioritizing can help you clarify your needs and values and make more informed decisions.

We All Need Relationships and Community

The stories of our lives are stories of connection. From birth to death we are in relationships; some we inherit and others we choose. We all need relationships and community to guide us through the opportunities and challenges of life. No one of us can be an island unto ourselves.

Time to Take Action

1. Make a list of three things you can do to strengthen your most important relationships.

2. Set a time within the next week to begin taking action on your list.

3. Ask someone to support you in making these changes.

Life Planning Network Chapter Contributors

Roberta K. Taylor, RNCS, MEd, Certified Senior Advisor, Life Planning/Retirement Coach, Co-author of *The Couple's Retirement Puzzle*, www.pathmaking.com, www.couplesretirementpuzzle.com. (Chapter Leader)

Sara Zeff Geber, PhD, Certified Retirement Options Coach, President of LifeEncore®, Author of *Fifty Plus, Minus Kids: Navigating Later Life without Adult Children*, www.LifeEncore.com.

Dorian Mintzer, MSW, PhD, BCC, Life Transition/Retirement Coach, Founder of Boomers and Beyond Special Interest Group, Co-author of *The Couples Retirement Puzzle*, www.revolutionizeretirement.com, www.couplesretirementpuzzle.com.

Resources

Marriage

Kelly Greene, "The 'Splitting' Headaches of Late-Life Divorce." The Wall Street Journal 6 Aug. 2011. <http://online.wsj.com>.

Laura S. Scott, *Two is Enough: A Couples Guide to Living Childless by Choice*, Seal Press, 2009.

Betty L. Polston, and Susan Goland, *Loving Mid-Life Marriage: A Guide to Keeping Romance Alive from the Empty Nest through Retirement*, John Wiley & Sons, 1999.

Roberta K. Taylor and Dorian Mintzer, *The Couples Retirement Puzzle: 10-Must Have Conversations for Transitioning to the Second Half of Life*, Lincoln Street Press, 2011.

Abigail Trafford, *As Time Goes By: Boomerang Marriages, Serial Spouses, Throwback Couples, and Other Romantic Adventures in an Age of Longevity*, Basic Books, 2010.

Adult Children

Jane Adams, *I'm Still your Mother: How to Get Along with your Grown-Up Children for the Rest of Your Life*, iUniverse.com, 1994.

Allison Bottke, *Setting Boundaries with your Adult Children: Six Steps to Hope and Healing for Struggling Parents*, Harvest House Publishers, 2008.

Ruth Nemzoff, *Don't Bite your Tongue, How to Foster Rewarding Relationships with your Adult Children*, Palgrave Macmillian, 2008.

Friendship

Connie Goldman, *Late Life Love: Romance & New Relationships in Later Years,* Fairview Press, 2006.

Irene S. Levine, *Best Friends Forever: Surviving a Break-Up with your Best Friend,* The Overlook Press, 2009.

Sandy Sheehy, *Connecting: The Enduring Power of Female Friendship,* William Morrow, 2000.

Community

Guide for Retirement Communities and "Best Places to Live:" www.cnnmoney.com/retirement

Homelink International: www.homelink.org

Website (free) to organize caregiving help: www.lotsahelpinghands.com

Retirement

John Cullinane and Cathy Fitzgerald, *The New Retirement: The Ultimate Guide to the Rest of Your Life,* Rodale, Inc., 2007.

Ellen Freudenheim, *Looking Forward: An Optimist's Guide to Retirement*, Stewart, Tabori & Chang, 2004.

Bill Roiter, *Beyond Work: How Accomplished People Retire Successfully*, John Wiley & Sons, 2008.

William Sadler and James Krefft, *Changing Course: Navigating Change After 50*, The Center for Third Age Leadership Press, 2007.

Martin E.P. Seligman, *Authentic Happiness*, Free Press by Simon & Schuster, 2002.

Bring Meaning to Money —
Financing your dreams

WHEN IT COMES TO MONEY, anxieties and concerns about the future are natural. The transition from paying our way primarily through our own labor to living mostly off pensions, Social Security and savings — whether this transition is by design or forced by circumstances — often means changes to both our interior and our exterior worlds.

Some of these changes are directly financial, but most of the others have financial implications. Whether your life is driven by dreams (which may need to be reality-tested against your finances) or by duties (such as caregiving), money will matter.

Most people, especially in the latter stages of life, agree that life should not be mostly about money. Ironically, though, the best way to make sure money does not dominate your life is to take the time to understand your finances, plan accordingly and keep your plan on track. This will reduce any anxieties you have about money, and enable you to move forward with confidence in dealing with the rest of your life.

So here is your formula for financial success:

DISCOVER — PLAN — LIVE™

DISCOVER

Start by identifying as much detail as you can about what you want in your future. Before you worry about the numbers and the dollars, focus on what *matters* to you, what gives you joy and adds meaning to your life. This book can help you answer the question, "What do I want the rest of my life to look like and be like?" Along the way, you'll also want to address, "What's coming up that I want and need to prepare for?"

Your New Financial Reality

Next, consider the financial context of your life, and how it might constrain you — or, perhaps, open up new opportunities.

From a financial standpoint, "retirement ain't what it used to be." Your dad's retirement probably included a decent pension, frequently improving Social Security benefits, a mortgage that was paid off by the time he retired, and most likely several children who could pitch in if things got bad. Your financial reality is likely to be different:

- Most jobs (except in government and education) do not offer traditional pensions any more. Instead they provide a 401(k) or other plan, usually with not nearly enough money in it, or in many cases, no retirement plan at all.

- Social Security benefits are more likely to be curtailed than improved over the remainder of your lifetime.

- People in your generation mostly have smaller families, and often have no children at all. If their money runs out (or they need care) they're more likely to be on their own.

- Meanwhile, life expectancies have continued to increase. Your money will probably need to last longer than your parents' money did.

- Although financial markets are unpredictable, the boom years could be over. The massive U.S. economic expansion of the post-World War era could slow down a lot, as baby boomers leave the workforce, and as nations like China and India try to grab the baton of industrial leadership. We can't be sure, but it might be harder to get good investment returns than it used to be.

None of this means you are doomed, financially. It only means that while the generation ahead of you could often get away with being on financial autopilot during retirement, you probably don't have that luxury. So you need to understand clearly whether your own circumstances put you ahead of the game, or behind.

Living with Uncertainty

Of course, none of us can be sure about where our own life is going, let alone where the outside world is going. The only thing we can be certain of, is that *uncertainty* isn't going anywhere. It's a permanent fixture of everyone's life, and if anything, it increases as we age. What matters is your ability to distinguish what you *can control* from that which you *cannot control*, and what's *important* from what's *unimportant*.

You don't know how long you've got, you don't know what the stock market will do, you don't know how the economy will evolve, what your health will be or what good or ill might befall your family. You can find yourself at the mercy of unanticipated challenges and unprepared for choices you must make.

Still, you can learn more about these and other financial risks, and you can sometimes insure against, help prevent or otherwise prepare to cope with these risks. Planning for and ultimately taking such steps not only puts you in a potentially better financial position, but improves your peace of mind.

Taking Inventory

Having considered the broader context, it's time to take inventory and determine how your available resources can best be used to support your future life. Confidence and security come from familiarity, and from new understandings of that which has been unfamiliar.

First, evaluate what your life looks like now. What elements do you want to keep, and what elements might you want to change? The *Bliss List** is a very powerful exercise, where you list the things you'd do for yourself, your family and others in a perfect world. Our *Goals and Major Expenditures (Time Line) Worksheet* (see Appendix D) can be similarly helpful as you think in more detail about specific elements that support your "bliss."

We have also provided a worksheet, *The Core Financial Pieces* (see Appendix E), to help you inventory the major financial elements you'll need to develop a financial plan. As you move through this inventory worksheet, think about your situation. Take the time to gather up your statements, information or documentation related to each section. This process will help you develop a more complete understanding of your financial situation, and will also prepare you well for working with a financial planner, if you choose to do so.

As you review each of the categories in *The Core Financial Pieces Worksheet*, note that you are looking for significance or irrelevance, strengths and gaps. Make notes about thoughts and questions that surface, as well as the emotions you experience while considering each of these areas.

You will observe some areas where you made great decisions. ("I borrowed money for education and it has really paid off. I love our home and our community—that was a smart decision!") Standing in this place, you'll be able to consider what changes you want to make to get your financial pieces aligned so they provide a supportive frame for the picture you've painted of the life you want to have.

---

* www.ccmiplan.com/Portals/0/CCMI_TheBlissListWorkbook.pdf

PLAN

Whatever your personal situation, planning for the things you want and can anticipate will help ensure you're in the best possible position to deal with what's ahead. Planning today allows all of us to improve our lives tomorrow and puts us in a stronger position to deal effectively with the unknown.

Not Just Planning, but "Financial Life Planning"

Financial Life Planning is the process of making the best use of your resources so that you can meet your needs today and in the future, and support cherished intentions and goals. It's a way to assure you have done what you can to support future activities that are meaningful, rewarding and significant. It isn't about finding "a number" or a particular investment, or investment return. No product can guarantee your security or abundance. Your abundance and ability to sustain a life of personal significance is the result of good decisions, made one after another in the face of realities that arise. The quality of your decisions improves when they are made within a context of understanding provided by a well-formed financial life plan.

Many significant financial questions go into the formation of such a plan. Each may be daunting on its own, even more so when one realizes the interrelatedness of these issues. Here are a few examples:

- How much do I need for retirement?

- Can I afford to be fully retired, or do I need to continue to earn money?

- When should I apply for my Social Security benefits?

- How should I invest my money?

- Do I need supplemental medical insurance on top of Medicare? Which one?

- Do I have the right mix of insurance, including long term care insurance?

- Do I need to scale down my living expenses?

- How do I prepare for the unexpected?

We have no universal answers to such questions, unfortunately. Each of us has different desires and priorities, different financial and other resources, different exposure to (and attitudes toward) risk, different constraints on what we can do or what we would feel comfortable doing. So we all need to create our own plan.

For some, it will be done passively and by default, at least until an event pushes a particular decision to the center of awareness. Waiting can severely decrease the options; however, it's never too late to take charge of the situation at hand by making the best choices from those that are still available. Regardless of what the future brings, we'll each be better off for having thought through our situations in advance.

Recent studies show that less than 50 percent of those over 50 years of age feel they are financially prepared for the future, yet the future is near. It doesn't need to be this way. Preparation is a key component for most positive outcomes, and always a part of optimal outcomes. Use our *Money Workbook Exercise* (see Appendix F) to help you along.

So now that you've completed your inventory, and are revved up to make sure your finances are in order, let's look at how you can create your financial life plan.

Should You Go It Alone?

Making decisions on the important questions and developing a plan for your future is something you can do on your own or with family members. You can also do it in collaboration with a financial planning professional, who has the experience and training to effectively guide you toward your goals.

For better or worse, most of us have a history of managing our own finances (or failing to), with only occasional help from outside. But most of us are not experts with money. There's no shame in that. Most of us also do not repair our own cars and appliances, do not make major repairs on our homes, or perform dental or surgical procedures on ourselves. Expertise has value.

It has particular value at this time of life. When you were young, with many years and perhaps many possible career paths in front of you, you had plenty of opportunities to make up for financial mistakes. But the longer you live, the less time and the fewer opportunities you have. If you make financial decisions now that lead you into trouble years from now, you'll have few or no good options to change course. So it's very important to make wise decisions now.

If you don't have the knowledge to make sound financial decisions, you still have options. You can consult with friends and family members, and pool your knowledge — but you may end up pooling misinformation, or end up with a lot of contradictory opinions or large gaps in knowledge that none of your acquaintances are equipped to bridge in a reliable fashion.

Fortunately, you have other resources, some of which are listed at the end of this chapter. Excellent books and websites provide both general and detailed information about financial issues in the latter stages of life. Software can help you make decisions about what might work in your particular situation.

There are limits though. Books, websites and software will not, by themselves, be able to integrate all the particulars of your finances with the dreams and desires you have for your own life. You may not be in a good position to supply this integration yourself, so you should at least consider seriously enlisting professional help.

Should You Work with a Financial Professional?

From a personal perspective, the intangible benefits of working with a professional planner are often immeasurable. These include peace of mind, a sense of security and optimism about the future that comes from knowing your "issues." From a financial perspective, tangible benefits can include higher net worth and more certain financial outcomes. Planners often play a pivotal role in reducing the "Behavior Gap," the financial losses individuals incur from their own "un-coached" behavior.

The issues you need to consider are these: How can you find someone who will give you good advice? What are you willing to pay? And can you find a planner that you feel understands you and is worthy of your trust? Here are some criteria you can use to reduce the field of potential candidates down to a final qualified few.

The first criterion is that of professional certification. You will find that there is no shortage of designations for individuals calling themselves financial planners, financial advisors, wealth managers and the like. One certification to look for is the Certified Financial Planner™ professional or CFP®. The CFP certification is to the financial planning profession what the CPA (or certified public accountant) is to the accounting industry. A professional who is a CFP has passed rigorous educational, testing and experience requirements. CFPs continue to meet continuing educational requirements, and as fiduciaries your interests always come first — they carry the highest duty of care under the law. A good way to find local CFP professionals is by using the "Find a Planner" tool at the Financial Planning Association website.

A major benefit of working with CFPs is that these professionals understand the many disciplines of personal finance and can coordinate with all of your other advisors (CPA, estate planning attorney, insurance provider, etc.) to ensure the cohesiveness of your plan. CFP professionals are more likely to provide a comprehensive, objective assessment with a "planning first" approach than some advisors carrying other designations.

Once you've identified one or more candidates for consideration, other criteria include understanding how each is paid, and what their biases are. It is important to understand that virtually all financial planners have biases. These arise in part from how they get paid, and from where they received their training or experience.

Financial people almost always get paid in one of three ways, or a combination:

- Commissions on the sale of financial products (e.g., insurance or mutual funds)

▓ Investment management fees (often based upon the dollar value of assets they manage)

▓ Hourly or flat-rate planning fees

Most advisors try not to put their own welfare first, but self-interest can have subtle influences on judgment. Commissions may influence advisors to recommend financial products that are not an ideal fit, or that don't work as well as competing products might. Investment management fees might lead an advisor to keep your assets in an investment fund when you perhaps would be better off using it to pay down debt, or for other purposes. Being paid a flat fee may encourage a planner to spend less time or go into less detail than is really needed, while getting paid an hourly rate may have the opposite effect.

If, like many people, you feel that someone receiving commissions will be less objective than one being paid an agreed upon fee, seek out a "fee only" planner. ("Fee based" planners receive both fees and commissions, and may be a sign the planner is moving towards the fee only model). Talk with each advisor about how they are paid, how much you are comfortable paying, and how you can keep the cost to that amount. One resource is the Garrett Planning Network, a network of hourly, fee only planners. Another is the National Association of Personal Financial Advisors, an association of fee only advisors.

Free help may be an option. The Financial Planning Association (FPA) has active chapters across the country providing planning advice and services to vulnerable middle and lower income households on a no-cost (pro bono) basis. At this writing, approximately two-thirds of all chapters are working on and organizing pro bono initiatives. Volunteers across the country are donating thousands of hours educating and planning for individuals in one-on-one and group settings. Planners contribute their time to develop personalized plans and help households make good financial decisions. More information is available at the Financial Planning Association website or by performing an Internet search including "Financial Planning Association," your city or county, and either "pro bono" or "Financial Planning Days" in the search criteria.

The FPA Pro Bono community often partners with other nonprofit organizations (i.e. senior centers, service organizations) in local communities to extend their reach and accessibility so check with your local FPA chapter and service organizations. The Financial Planning Association encourages the use of "Letters of Engagement" stating the advice is free, products are not being sold, and you are not to be solicited for paid business. Be wary of others offering free advice without signed statements.

Many financial professionals earned their spurs in the investment or the insurance business, while others came up through banking, accounting or some other path. Whatever their path, their experience usually improves their feelings toward the branch of the industry they are rooted in, with an opposite effect toward competing branches. You should understand where your advisor came from, and take account of it in your own decisions.

It's also useful to know that most financial professionals have areas of expertise and "niches" which they are most proficient at serving, and it may not be in helping people like you. Of those who do have that expertise, some may be good at crunching numbers, but not at figuring out how to make your life better. Or you might just not click with them for other reasons.

So how do you find the right professional to help *you*?

■ Ask people you know and trust for a referral — someone who helped *them*.

■ Look for people with appropriate professional designations, such as Certified Financial Planner (CFP).

■ Understand forms of compensation and your preference.

■ Interview prospective advisors to determine how well they fit with your planning needs, pocket book and communication style.

When meeting, ask them questions. Are their clients similar to you in age, wealth, employment, aspirations? Do the planners have experience in assisting clients with needs similar to yours? Do you need assistance with employment benefits, special needs, stock options or family needs? Can they tell you how they've assisted others and what some of the challenges may be, or how they might address them? Be sure you are comfortable with the comments they make, and in the way they are made. Advice should not be the first thing they provide. You will want to choose a planner who is focused on developing an understanding of who you are before they provide advice.

The Certified Financial Planner Board of Standards* provides additional information on how to choose a planner, as does NAPFA.

And however you develop your financial plan, don't hesitate to get a second opinion if you have any doubts.

LIVE

The final step to financial success is to live — but to do so differently, using the knowledge you have gained from the planning process, and the plan itself, to *defend* your future against financial disruptions, and to *enable* yourself to make your future life into what you want it to be.

Putting Money in Its Place

Some folks avoid financial planning because they know they're in for bad news. Others think they're doing okay, but find out otherwise as they work through their plan. If you fit one of these categories, don't give up! Most people who engage in a planning process find that they can have anything they want — they just can't have *everything* they want.

If you are in the second half of your life, you probably have already learned that life is not about money. Yes, money matters, but if you have to compromise on account of limited financial resources, you can still have a fulfilling, engaging, wonderful life.

Focus your resources on what matters. Figure out what is truly most important to you. For most people, it comes down to what

---

* Request *Consumer Guide to Financial Planning* at
  www.cfp.net/learn/requestkit.asp

they do, whom they do it with and the environment in which all that occurs. Sometimes spiritual values are central. As we age, we care more about finding ways to help others, and pass along our wisdom. Most of these things don't require much money. And for those that do, take care of the ones that mean the most to you, and let the others go.

If you are *far* short of financial resources, you need to see if you can find ways to earn more income or to reduce your expenses. One of the best ways to reduce expenses is to share living space with family or friends — everyone saves a lot of money, and enjoys the benefits of companionship and having helping hands nearby. See our discussions on work, housing, community, lifestyles and relationships in the chapters entitled: "The Relationship Dividend," "Good Work," and "The Right Place."

> Going forward, assume you will live a long life and that the economy will continue to be volatile. Revisit your plan frequently, so it reflects and changes with your life. The primary purpose of your plan is to support what you deem important, and to provide context for your decision making.

A satisfying, fulfilling life is part art and part science. It's important to blend both the unique personal aspects of ourselves (the qualitative aspects) with our resources and realities of the world we live in (the quantitative aspects). Our ideal future lies where our highest callings and most important priorities are supported and encouraged by our means and resources.

Life Planning Network Chapter Contributors

Bradley T. Baumann, CFP®, Certified Financial Planner™, Sudden Money® Advisor, www.CCMIPlan.com, www.BradBaumann.com.

Elizabeth W. Jetton, CFP®, Financial Planner, Consultant and Educator, www.DirectionsforWomen.com, www.ElizabethJetton.com.

Chuck Yanikoski, Retirement Adviser,
www.ChuckYRetirement.com.

Resources

Money

Rick Kahler and Kathleen Fox, *Conscious Finance: Uncover Your Hidden Money Beliefs and Transform the Role of Money in Your Life*, FoxCraft, Inc., 2007.

George Kinder, *The Seven Stages of Money Maturity: Understanding the Spirit and Value of Money in Your Life*, Dell, 2000.

Ted Klontz, Brad Klontz and Rick Kahler, *The Financial Wisdom of Ebenezer Scrooge: 5 Principles to Transform Your Relationship with Money*, HCI, 2008.

Financial Planning

Doug Lennick and Kathleen Jordan, *Financial Intelligence: How to Make Smart, Values-Based Decisions with Your Money and Your Life*, FPA Press, 2010.

John E. Nelson and Richard N. Bolles, *What Color Is Your Parachute? for Retirement: Planning a Prosperous, Healthy, and Happy Future*, Ten Speed Press, 2010.

Mitch Anthony, *New Retirementality: Planning Your Life and Living Your Dreams... at Any Age You Want*, Wiley & Sons, 2008.

www.letsmakeaplan.org/ — The consumer website of CFP Board of Standards.

www.ssa.gov/ — Social Security website.

For Women

Eleanor Blayney, *Women's Worth: Finding Your Financial Confidence*, Direction$, LLC, 2010.

Alan B. Ungar and Brad Baumann, *Financial Self-Confidence for the Suddenly Single: A Woman's Guide*, Lowell House Press, Updated 2011. Now available as a free eBook www.ccmiplan.com/RESOURCES/Books.aspx

www.directionsforwomen.com — An initiative to empower, educate and engage women around money.

Wiser's Financial Planning Workbook — Tools from the Women's Institute for a Secure Retirement (www.wiserwomen.org/images/imagefiles/wiserFinanPlanWkbkOct.2011.pdf).

Advisors and Planners

www.fpanet.org/ — The consumer website of the Financial Planning Association, the organization that fosters the value of financial planning and advances the financial planning profession. "Find a planner search" available.

www.NAPFA.org — The website of the National Association of Personal Financial Advisors, a membership organization of fee-only financial advisors.

www.GarrettPlanningNetwork.com — An international network of fee-only financial advisors and planners.

www.ncoa.org/assets/files/pdf/savvy-saving-seniors/Savvy-Saving-Seniors-Participant-Handbook-FINAL.pdf Savvy Saving Seniors Handbook. For many vulnerable and disadvantaged older adults, the path to economic security begins with basic money management. This workbook gives tips on good money skills including how to budget, avoid scams, and apply for benefits that can help them stay secure and independent longer.

Good Work —
Discover what work works for you

"Whether for free, for a fee, for community, for fun or full-time,
part-time, or in response to just-in-time needs,
good work is work that works for you!"
— Carleen MacKay

ONCE UPON A TIME IN THE 1840S, hoards of hard-working people began a rush to California with big dreams of striking it rich in the gold fields! But, did they succeed? Did they line their sweaty pockets with gold?

A very few did through demanding labor in tough, primitive mining camps with names like Hangtown and Hell's Delight.

But ... history tells us that the people who prospered during the gold rush years were those who saw an alternative to doing the backbreaking work. These smart folks *saw another way*. They supplied the miners with their picks and shovels and, subsequently, invested their profits in land and emerging businesses.

Ah ... the gold rush entrepreneurs .... those resilient souls succeeded, those who did not follow the blindingly obvious and harder, grueling work of most miners ... those who *"saw another way."*

The moral of the story is that the smartest people, then and now, find alternatives to the well-trodden paths the masses follow.

Welcome to the 21st century's gold rush — a rush to live longer, better and healthier and, for most of us, to continue to work, in some capacity, long beyond some chronologically imposed date. This is a moment in time when and where, for a variety of reasons, work is regarded differently than it was a few scant years ago when "jobs" were the only way most people defined work.

Sometimes, but far from always, work is a job – much like the job you have now or the job you once held. Other times, the career or job you once held is no longer available or ... the work itself is so materially changed that it's not available to you! And, sometimes, you may simply want to do something different for reasons of your own!

If you want, or need, to continue to work in some capacity, you're in the right place at the right time of your life. We'll show you how to turn threats into opportunities and how to begin to leverage workplace changes to your advantage in the 21st early century!

Journey with us as you get ready for your future. Follow our **Eight-Step Planning Strategy for Boomers***, an easy, sequential strategic planning model. As you work through the eight steps, you are encouraged to refer to the recommended books, authors and websites in the Resources list at the end of the chapter.

The Steps

8 — Marketing Tool Kit
7 — Your Plan
6 — Challenges & Barriers
5 — Your Career Options
4 — Today's Hot Opportunities
3 — Marketplace Trends
2 — Internal Analysis
1 — Letting Go

---

* The Eight-Step Planning Strategy for Boomers is copyrighted by Carleen MacKay and Brad Taft. Go to www.agelessinamerica.com and click on *Plan "B" for Boomers* for more details about the 8-step strategy.

Step 1 — Letting Go

"When I let go of what I am, I become what I might be."
—Lao Tzu

Today, a few moments before her 80th birthday, Jan Hively, founding director of the Vital Aging Network and expert on letting go of the past and transforming expectations for aging, says that she's been happier during the last decade than at any other time in her life.

"I've been walking my talk! I love the sense of independence and freedom," says Hively, "that comes along with being responsible for my own life — and for no one else's. I've followed my passions to meaningful work that I plan to pursue through my last breath. Most important, I've learned to listen to myself as well as others, and to 'let go.'"

We all know people who are stuck in houses filled with stuff because they can't face throwing away objects collected in the past that offer memories and identity. We also know lots of people who say that they're so busy with their daily schedule that they can't move on to start something new. It stands to reason that the first step to making change is to make room for change.

Especially as we grow older, we want life to be productive but also simpler, not busier. Whether it's furniture or daily activities, "stuff" is a barrier to positive change.

"Beyond the physical," says Hively, "my 'stuff' has included trying to control what other people are doing, resentments about what they haven't done, fear about lots of things such as lack of income and loss of status, and grief about all the losses that come naturally with aging.

"My routine for 'letting go' is to face what's going on that is generating negative feelings and apply the Serenity Prayer. *'Give me the serenity to accept what I cannot change, the courage to change what I can, and the wisdom to know the difference.'*"

All of us must adapt to the rapid shifts of the global economy and America's changing status within it. For those of us in midlife and beyond, this means letting go of career expectations shaped by the industrial economy we grew up in.

Is it time for you to let go of old expectations, whether shaped by the ego or past experience?

Step 2 — Internal Analysis

"Wholly unprepared, we take the step into the afternoon [or second half] of life. Worse still, we take this step with the false assumption that our truths and ideals will serve as before. But we cannot live the afternoon of life according to the program of life's morning, for what was great in the morning will be little at evening, and what in the morning was true will at evening have become a lie."
— *Carl Jung*

Nothing is constant. The growth we experience in mid and later life brings new priorities, perspectives, needs and skills. Hence, a thorough self-analysis may be even more essential at this time of life than in earlier years because the familiar script will no longer describe who we are today.

Are you stuck trying to determine what you want to do next?

One of the most important steps in the process is beginning at the beginning with an internal analysis.

An efficient and proven three-part framework for internal analysis has assisted midlife career changers and boomers to determine their top five values, top five skills, and their passions. Examine your values, skills and passions by following the links below. The process will actually be easy and fun!

1. **Values:** Check out the "Career Thought Leaders" blog by Elizabeth Craig to learn about the importance of determining your foundational core values.

The University of Minnesota provides a card sort exercise that helps you analyze what you value — everything from collaboration, decision-making, and creativity, to growth, learning and flexibility.

What we spend our time on tends to be what we value. Are you bringing your values to your life and work?

2. **Skills:** Through many experiences, you have acquired a large number of capabilities that you enjoy doing for work and play. Taking a moment to look back at those enjoyable natural abilities and skills provides insight into what your next work could be.

   An often-overlooked, yet highly useful approach to looking at things you enjoy, is to make a list of positions you've held. For this exercise, a "position" refers to both paid and unpaid activities and work. Draw a line down the center of a blank piece of paper. For each position, list what you "liked" on one side, and on the other side list "dislikes." As you continue this exercise, distinct skills and passions you have enjoyed over time will emerge. Check out the University of Minnesota's card sort assessment on skills.

3. **Passions:** What gets you up in the morning and energizes you to begin your day? Paying attention is the key element in determining your passions. What are you doing when you are so fully engaged that you lose all track of time?

For more valuable tools to help you identify your values and strengths, check out the introductory chapter of this book, "Your Life Lessons."

Now that you understand your core values, skills, abilities and passions, decide what you want to offer the world. And please remember that the "work" you are preparing for may include meaningful volunteer, civic, and philanthropic activities as well as paid work. Your "work" may involve learning, for learning itself is "work" and, some might say, our most important work.

Echoing the importance of internal analysis, Renee Lee Rosenberg says in her book, *Achieving the Good Life After 50*, "Becoming aware of who you are, what you see, your experiences, your skills, your assumptions, your influences, your self-perceptions, is essential in the quest for taking responsibility for yourself and dealing successfully with changes that are taking place within your life."

Once you've analyzed your values, skills and passions, you can align them with today's marketplace.

Step 3 — Marketplace Trends

"Don't seek comfort in your ticket on the last train to the good times. The station has already been converted to a hybrid car sales outlet."

— *Brad Tipler, a San Diego Futurist*

Bonds between employers and employees have grown weaker; the global workforce is a reality; technological innovations profoundly impact how and where we work today and where we will work, or not work, tomorrow.

The good news is that the market always signals the work changes of which you must be aware. Daily indicators come from demographic shifts, increased competition from abroad, technological innovation and thrilling new inventions.

There is every reason to study anticipated changes in markets because people, like industries, businesses and educational institutions, who do not change to meet the demands of the marketplace, are at high risk of being left behind on the scrapheap of time.

"Anyone with access to the Internet and the Web can become self-educated in all manner of subjects." Good advice from Frederick Lynch, a government professor at Claremont McKenna College, in his book, *One Nation under AARP.* A timely study of the boomer demographic, it's an easy starting point in your quest for market knowledge.

If you wish to learn more about emerging market trends, go online to Wikipedia. Likewise, go to Google, enter "set up alerts" in the search column and insert key words that describe your areas of interest. Every time articles are published about the subject matter you have identified, your inbox will "alert" you.

Step 4 — Today's "Hot" Opportunities

... just remember that what is "hot" today may be cold tomorrow!

Demographic, technological, economic, societal and global changes carry with them both threats and opportunities. Embedded in each of the following highlighted changes are opportunities for work, jobs, services and new products.

Boomer/Senior Products and Services — 77-78 million boomers, and close to 10,000 people turning 65 each and every day, make the right products and services for these large groups a sure thing!

Consignment Store Sales — When consumer confidence is down, consignment sales are up!

Ethics Officers — Think Bernie Madoff.

Health Care — Many areas of health care services are expanding as our nation ages.

Homeland Security — No, the world is not a safer place.

New Products — Opportunities abound especially in the medical devices and wellness fields.

Part-Time, Temporary and Free Agent Careers — These industries will continue to boom for the prepared. And, with up to a third of federal and state workers retiring over the next few years, you'll find temporary work for workers in all sectors of the economy.

Pet Services and Products — Need we say more?

Tutoring — We need tutors in all areas of learning for all ages and stages.

Social Purpose Work, Including Volunteering — For many people, giving back is the key to living the good life. As a starting point, take a look at Encore.org and the programs and organizations listed there to help folks find pathways to meaningful service. Encore work combines passion, purpose and, in many cases, a paycheck.

For additional ideas, go to The U.S. Bureau of Labor Statistics online and search for articles about "Tomorrow's Jobs."

AgelessinAmerica.com lets you access several books and products that describe dozens of additional opportunities for work in the second decade of the 21st century.

Step 5 — Your Career Options

Remember our gold miners' story about the people who succeeded well beyond the miners' back-breaking work efforts? Let us, together, *see new ways to work*!
    You can work as a:

Temp or a Free Agent. Did you know that temporary agencies offer opportunities at all levels of experience and that they are one of the fastest growing businesses in the U.S.? Some people look to temporary agencies for marketing assistance. Others prefer a free agency, and market, bill and provide services themselves without the help of a temporary agency. Daniel Pink's book, *Free Agent Nation*, makes compelling arguments for this choice.

Specialist or Subject-Matter Expert. Do you specialize in meeting high marketplace needs for organizations at times of startup, turn-around or rapid expansion? If so, it's time to learn more about the growing world of these highly specialized experts. Go to the Turn-around Management Association. Or, contact your local SCORE office for more about this way to work.

Franchisee. This is another fast growing option for boomers who seek to create a five-year plan in order to phase into retirement or who want to help secure the financial future for a son, daughter or grandchild (these are called "Daddy Deals," by the way). You may be surprised by the many options and costs. Check out Frannet.com as well as other franchise networks on the Internet.

Portfolio Manager. Like the familiar stock portfolio, a work port folio *diversifies* your approach by managing a variety of options in order to achieve early return, personal security or satisfaction as well as long-term gain. For example, you might volunteer in a new field, take a class, take on project assignments through your existing (or previous) employer in order to ensure some income flow as you reposition for the future. David Corbett's book, *Portfolio Life,* is a useful tool.

Volunteer, Civic or Philanthropic Contributor. These activities offer a new "career" direction and a new opportunity for making an impact, starting where you are today and evolving as your interests and level of commitment to an issue, or a cause, shift over time. Volunteers who provide pro-bono help to a non-profit while searching for other work, may find a new direction in the form of encore work in the social or civic sectors. See Encore.org for additional information.

How else are the *smart* people working today? Let us count a few of the many ways ... (1) as advisory board members to struggling start-ups, (2) as virtual workers, (3) as tutors to children, (4) as coaches, (5) in nonprofits, (6) as new business entrepreneurs, (7) as small business owners, (8) as part-timers and (9) in *101 Weird Ways to Make Money,* by Steve Gillman. Want to know more about the many ways to work in your maturity? Google it!

Step 6 — Challenges and Barriers*

The challenges and barriers you face are what keep most people from reaching their full potential. For example, when you think about meeting a *challenge* does it make you think of *summoning your courage* for what lies ahead? Or, does the word itself suggest possibilities of a blind, terrifying leap into a deep and dark abyss?

There is nothing to stop you from meeting challenges but fear itself and, often, the most challenging fears have to do with the specter of age discrimination. Overcome the fear-provoking myths and biases with facts and tips about the advantages maturity offers. Take a look at the Flash Card Set of Myths at AgelessInAmerica.com, complete with facts and tips for dealing with age biases.

Remember that fear causes people to retreat to the familiar even when they should rise up to meet the demands of the future. In other words, challenge is usually fear with a dollop of ignorance thrown into the mix.

When you think of the word *barrier*, think of it as a missing skill, or an educational gap, or a learning task you must undertake in order to realize your goals. In other words, a barrier is something in your

---

* Excerpted, in part, from *Plan "B" for Boomers,* by Carleen Mackay, co-founder of Ageless in America, and the San Diego Workforce Partnership.

background that will preclude you from getting the work you want until you fill in the "gap" with what an employer or a client needs.

You are challenged with acknowledging a future as unlike your past as your maturity is to your childhood ... and then ... to see hidden within every sound bite of economic news, the new opportunities that await you when you're ready to move forward.

In terms of overcoming barriers because of skills or educational gaps, consider continuing education programs offered by your local community colleges or extended education programs at four-year institutions. Consider schools, such as National University in the West, that specialize in online education. Look into the Osher Life-long Learning Institute. Osher offers university quality, non-credit courses to adults 50 and better. The University of Phoenix is the choice for people who prefer to learn in person or online from working experts. Check out the "Plus 50 Initiatives" from the American Association of Community Colleges to determine if your hometown offers this program. There is no shortage of options in each and every community and no shortage of price points for you to consider. It is powerful to learn and even more powerful to position recent learning experiences with prospective employers or clients. Overcome the myth that "*You can't teach old dogs new tricks.*" Learn some new tricks! You'll be surprised at the strength you can leverage when you learn something new.

Step 7 — Your Plan

"If you don't know where you are going,
you might wind up someplace else."
— Yogi Berra

A SMART plan, the essence of good planning, needs to be written, and Specific, Measurable, Action-oriented, Realistic and Time-framed.

Before you write your plan, review your work. Have you completed every step of the recommended process? If so, you are ready to force-rank your few top interests in order of preference as these become your goals and objectives that form the basis of smart planning.

Finally, review your plan with a respected critic who will help you fill in missing pieces.

Step 8 - Marketing Toolkit

Marketing tools give life to your campaign

If your tactics begin and end with developing a ho-hum chrono-logical resume, you have missed exploring and taking strategic advantage of developing an array of 21st century marketing tools.

Alphabetically, some of these tools include: biographies, blogs, branding statements, business cards, business networks, cover letters, e-mail correspondence, newsletters, resumes, sales proposals, social networks (LinkedIn, Facebook, Twitter), websites and vimeos. A great deal is written throughout the web about all of these tools, but allow us to add information about just two of these you may not have considered for your toolkit.

Websites. Did you know that you can buy a website template for a very modest cost? A website, unlike a resume or a biography, adds depth to your experience and background. It also demonstrates your comfort with the use of technology. Intuit's template is one such tool. Go to AgelessinAmerica.com to see an example of Intuit's easy and affordable way to utilize their template design.

Vimeos. Are vimeos new to you? They are one of the latest tools to add to your toolkit or to augment your website. Vimeos, or videos, are short visual presentations that present your information in compelling ways. Many people take the time to watch an interesting video; other people will read your website, each according to their own preferred learning style.

Check out an example of a vimeo that expands upon and summarizes the **Eight Step Planning Strategy for Boomers** we just covered in this chapter. It will critically increase your knowledge about work at this career stage. (Go to www.AgelessinAmerica.com and click on the link to the vimeo.)

Life Planning Network Chapter Contributors

Carleen MacKay, Director Mature Workforce Initiatives, Career Partners International. Author of *Plan "B" for Boomers, The 50,000 Mile Checkup*, and *WORK* (in press). Co-author of *Return of the Boomers, Boom or Bust,* and *Myth Cards,* www.agelessinamerica.com. (Chapter Leader)

Elizabeth Craig, MBA, MCDP, CCM, Master Career and Job Search Strategist, Speaker and Consultant, www.elcglobal.com.

Joanne Hadlock, EdD, NCCC, Counseling Psychologist, Nationally Certified Career Consultant, www.joannehadlock.us.

Jan Hively, PhD, Co-founder of the Vital Aging Network, www. vital-aging-network.org, the Minnesota Creative Arts and Aging Network, www.mncaan.net, and the SHiFT Network, www.shiftonline.org.

Mary Radu, MS, MSW, CPCC, Certified Professional Coach, Philanthropy Mentor and author of the *The Roadmap to Meaningful Midlife*®, www.pathmakercoaching.com.

Renee Lee Rosenberg, MA, LMHC, Author of *Achieving the Good Life After 50: Tools and Resources for Making It Happen,* Certified Five O'Clock Club Master Coach and Retirement Specialist, www.retirementutor.com, www.positivitypro.com.

Resources

Self and Market Assessment

Marcus Buckingham, *Go Put Your Strengths to Work*, Free Press, 2007.

Elizabeth Craig, "Values! The Foundational Core of Working Your Purpose," www.careerthoughtleaders.com/blog/author/elizabeth-craig.

Kerry Hannon, *What's Next? Follow Your Passion and Find Your Dream Job*, Chronicle Books, 2010.

Frederick Lynch, *One Nation under AARP*, University of California Press, 2012.

Carleen MacKay, *The 50,000 Mile Mid-career Check-up*, and *Plan B for Boomers & Beyond* (free e-books).

Overcoming Myths About Older Workers, flash cards, www.agelessinamerica.com/products.html.

Daniel Pink, *Drive: The Surprising Truth About What Motivates Us*, Penguin Books, 2009.

Paul D. Tieger and Barbara Barron, *Do What You Are: Discover the Perfect Career for You Through the Secrets of Personality Type*, Little, Brown and Company, 2007.

University of Minnesota, "Value Sort", http://oca.cce.umn.edu/prototypes/cardsort/values.

University of Minnesota, "Skill Sort", http://oca.cce.umn.edu/prototypes/cardsort/skills.

Work Options and Readiness

Marci Alboher, *The Encore Career Handbook*, Workman, 2013.

American Association of Community Colleges, Plus 50 ageless learning programs, http://plus50.aacc.nche.edu.

David Corbett and Richard Higgins, *Portfolio Life: The New Path to Work, Purpose and Passion After 50*, Jossey-Bass, 2006.

Encore careers, www.encore.org/find.

FRANNET, franchise consultants, www.frannet.com.

Kerry Hannon, *AARP Great Jobs for Everyone 50+: Finding Work That Keeps You Happy and Healthy ... And Pays the Bills*, 2012.

Marc Freedman, *Encore: Finding Work That Matters in the Second Half of Life*, Public Affairs, 2007.

Steve Gillman, *101 Weird Ways to Make Money*, Wiley, 2011.

Barbara Moses, *What Next? The Complete Guide to Taking Control of Your Working Life*, and *Dish: Midlife Women Tell the Truth about Work, Relationships and the Rest of Life*, Dorling Kindersley, 2003.

Osher Lifelong Learning Institute, list of programs, www.usm.maine.edu/olli/national/map.jsp

Daniel Pink, *Free Agent Nation: The Future of Working For Yourself*, Warner Books, 2002.

Renee Rosenberg, *Achieving the Good Life After 50: Tools and Resources for Making It Happen*, Five O'Clock Books, 2007.

SCORE, small business counseling and mentoring, www.score.org.

Turnaround Management Association, corporate renewal industry, www.turnaround.org.

US Bureau of Labor Statistics, www.bls.gov (to research work options, type "tomorrow's jobs" in the search field)

Work Search

AARP Work Reimagined, jobs — discussions — news, http://workreimagined.aarp.org.

Jobs Over 50, source for hiring baby boomers & retirees, http://jobsover50.com.

Retirement Jobs, jobs for people over 50, www.retirementjobs.com.

Seniors4Hire, career center for folks 50 and older, Retired Brains, http://retirementjobs.retiredbrains.com.

Workforce 50, employment and career change resources for people over 50, www.workforce50.com.

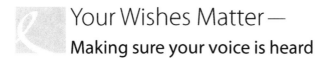

Your Wishes Matter—
Making sure your voice is heard

AS YOU MOVE THROUGH this book and explore ways to live smart in the second half of your life—like the areas of work, adventure, relationships and community—you'll find that you also need to be smart about planning for the legal and security side of things. This chapter will help you think about some of the practical steps you need to take to secure the future you want for you and your family. We'll focus on how you can:

- Simplify passing your estate to loved ones

- Protect against the high cost of long-term health care

- Authorize others to make financial or medical decisions if you become unable to do so yourself

- Qualify for an array of public benefits (Medicare, Medicaid, Veterans benefits, Social Security, etc.)

- Protect against scams, abuses and financial exploitation

- Lessen the chance that your estate plan will be challenged

In short, we'll concentrate on what you can do to lower the threats of uncertainty to your ability to enjoy other aspects of your life.

Why You Need Legal Planning

Sound legal planning begins by recognizing that most of us will live a lot longer than our parents. Longer life seems desirable, but it doesn't change the fact that most of us will at some point face diminishing capacities, chronic illness, the loss of loved ones and other events we would usually prefer not to think about. It's just those kinds of uncertainties for which legal planning helps us prepare.

Because there are strict but changing rules for things like taxes, estates and long-term care, lawyers can be useful guides to what at first can seem impossibly complex. In fact, there is now a legal specialty that deals with these issues. The terms "elder law" and "elder law attorney" were coined in the late 1980s, when lawyers (and others) became aware that longer lives were reshaping our society and called for new legal tools.

Until then, people worked with "estate planners" to discuss what effects estate and gift taxes would have on the money they passed to their children or to charities. But now that federal estate taxes apply only to couples with more than $10 million and individuals with more than $5 million (at least through 2012), plans to reduce estate taxes are largely irrelevant for most Americans.

This chapter is directed to the 99 percent of Americans who need to focus on more basic concerns: whether they will outlive their savings, how they will meet the rapidly escalating costs of nursing home care if that becomes necessary, who can make important decisions concerning their money and health if their mental abilities decline and, if so, whom to trust.

Elder law attorneys work closely with life planners, financial advisers, geriatric care managers and others to design "holistic" approaches to issues that can be both complicated and emotional. You can find lawyers trained in this elder law specialty at the National Academy of Elder Law Attorneys (NAELA) website.

New and Old Ideas about Estate Planning

Estate Planning Issues	Old Ideas	New Ideas
Wills and Trusts	A will is sufficient because it outlines how your assets will be allocated	You also need a Health Care Proxy (HCP), Durable Power of Attorney (DPOA) and a plan
Taxes	Federal estate taxes will eat up your legacy	Federal estate taxes no longer apply to most couples and individuals
Probate	Probate should be avoided at any cost	Careful planning can remove the need for probate, but avoiding it may come at its own expense
Transitions	Not usually addressed	Joint accounts, beneficiary designations, DPOAs and HCPs
Long-Term Care	Not usually addressed	Long-Term Care Insurance (LTCI) or Medicaid offer protection
Outliving Assets	Shorter lives, lower costs, Social Security and pensions are sufficient	Longer lives, inflation, limited savings, fewer pensions raise the threat; Social Security covers less

Taking Retirement Benefits

The decision to retire used to be simple (and often mandatory), at least for those who worked for large companies with pension plans. For most workers, 65 used to be the magic number, the age of retirement created by German Chancellor Bismark in the 1870s and adopted by the U.S. Social Security Administration over 75 years ago. It made sense when average life expectancy was lower than 65, when much of labor was physically draining, when most who reached 65 were already battling chronic diseases, and when most work ended with mandatory retirements.

Of course, none of that is typical today. In a time when some people retire before age 65 but many more continue working into their 70s and beyond, the decision about when to take retirement benefits is a personal one. And with many options and implications, these decisions need to be made carefully.

Medicare is the only retirement benefit that automatically becomes available at age 65, though it is possible to defer the parts that pay for medical services (Part B) and prescription drugs (Part D) until later. Opting into these coverages after age 65 can only be done at certain times. Since Medicare doesn't cover all health care expenses, most people purchase supplemental (Medigap) policies. The cost of these policies has nearly doubled in the past decade, leading many to stay in company health plans, if available, as long as possible.

MORE INFORMATION ON MEDICARE AND SOCIAL SECURITY

An excellent description of Medicare coverage choices is available on the Medicare website. Social Security options are explained at the Social Security site.

Social Security can be taken as early as age 62 with a reduced benefit. It can also be taken after age 65. The decision about when to begin Social Security should be discussed with your financial advisor as well as your lawyer since it involves assumptions about your savings and other resources, such as a company or public pension. This decision can also be affected by how much money you continue to earn from paid work.

Since Social Security is not likely to keep pace with inflation, particularly for baby boomers who have not yet qualified, most of us will have to rely on income from our 401(k) plans, IRAs and other retirement savings. Yet, the stock market, in which most of these plans invest, is uncertain and lower-risk investments (such as bonds and CDs) may fail to cover future inflation. Learning to live on less money will become a necessary skill for most of us.

Paying for Long-Term Health Care

Even if you have saved prudently, invested wisely and budgeted well, the greatest threat to a secure financial future is the possibility that you or a spouse may require long-term care. At least 70 percent of people over age 65 will require long-term care at some point in their lives. The cost of nursing home care (or, for that matter, 24/7 care at home) would eventually bankrupt most Americans. Imagine adding $10,000 to $13,000 *a month* to your budget.

Medicare, Medigap insurance and HMO plans only cover the *initial* cost of post-hospital care. They are not designed to cover more than 100 days and rarely pay for more than 20 days of care after a hospital stay.

WHO PAYS FOR LONG-TERM CARE?

Medicare: NO
Health Insurance: NO
Your Funds: YES
Long-Term Care Insurance (LTCI): YES
Medicaid: YES

Other than drawing down your savings, there is just one way to avoid the potential for exorbitant long-term care bills: buying long-term care insurance (LTCI). About 30 insurers in the U.S. offer LTCI at a constant cost based on your age when you purchase the policy. In principle, the cost in the first month is the same 10 years later.

Most long-term care policies cover room, board and other care provided in a nursing home as well as special care at home or in assisted living facilities. Policies provide as little as $100 a day to more than $400 a day toward the cost of care. When buying LTCI, keep these factors in mind:

1. Choose the daily benefit that, along with personal resources, will cover qualified in-home care and nursing home costs not only now but in the future.

2. Select a company that will be financially able to meet its future obligations.

3. Pick a company that is likely to accept you as a policyholder. Most companies sell policies to people up to 80 years old, but premiums rise rapidly the older you are when you obtain a policy. "Individual" policies (which are regulated by state insurance commissions) are available only to persons the companies consider less likely to require long-term care. Such "underwriting" eliminates between one-third to one-half of applicants from any coverage at all.

People with limited resources shouldn't purchase LTCI if they won't be able to pay premiums continually. Failure to pay premiums will make the policy "lapse" and lapsed policies are worthless. Consider whether, at age 65, for example, you're prepared to pay premiums of, say, $6,000 a year *for 30 years*!

Most people in nursing homes will at some point depend on Medicaid to cover at least some of their expenses. Medicaid, the state-federal program available to people who cannot afford nursing home expenses, was designed for the "medically needy." This is defined as persons whose medical expenses exceed their income and savings. In most cases, your residence, personal property, business property (including rental property), and money set aside for funeral arrangements are not counted when calculating income and savings.

In 2012, that means that people in nursing homes may qualify for Medicaid by reducing their "countable" assets to $2,000 if single or about $114,000 for a married couple if one spouse is still living in the community. Lawyers who specialize in Medicaid planning can help you determine if you can safely transfer assets or re-characterize assets (for example, converting a vacation home to an income-producing rental property).

Planning for Incapacity

At some time in our lives, many of us will be incapacitated, requiring that health care or financial decisions be made for us. Unless you make arrangements ahead of time, transferring authority over health care and financial decisions requires court appointment of a Guardian (for health care decisions) and Conservator (for financial decisions).

Courts won't make such appointments until it is clear, based on medical evidence, that a person can no longer make those decisions and that the individual recommended to make decisions in their place is fully capable of doing so. "Interested parties," usually a spouse and children, must be notified and, in a growing number of states, a plan must be presented to the court on the care to be given to the incapacitated person.

The problem with this is that the process is public, it can be expensive, it wastes critical time (especially during crises) and it introduces uncertainty if members of the family oppose a particular appointment or argue over whether a person really needs a Guardian or Conservator.

All this can be avoided simply by executing two basic documents:

1) Durable Power of Attorney (naming someone to carry out financial transactions)

2) Health Care Proxy or, in some states, a Durable Power of Attorney for Health Care Decisions (appointing someone to make health care decisions).

It is best to name at least one alternate to serve if the first choice is not available or able to carry out his or her functions when needed. Based on our experiences with several difficult situations, we urge you not to name two or three people to serve simultaneously.

DURABLE POWERS OF ATTORNEY

- You can choose whether a Durable Power of Attorney can be used immediately (without necessarily forfeiting your own authority) or be "springing," deferring authority until you express your desire for it to take effect or when a physician decides that it needs to take effect.

- Durable Powers of Attorney should list all the authorities that might be needed to plan for the time when you can no longer manage your own affairs. Since the goal is to avoid the cost, delay and contention of going to court, a good Durable Power of Attorney should address a great number of issues – the right to make gifts for tax or other purposes, placing assets into existing trusts, appealing public benefits decisions, dealing directly with certain insurers and stock brokers, etc.

- Durable Powers of Attorney should be refreshed every two years or so, because some banks and other third parties ignore documents they consider stale.

HEALTH CARE PROXIES

- Most Health Care Proxies are "springing," which means that authority is not transferred until a physician writes an opinion that you are no longer capable of making rational, knowledgeable medical decisions.

- Privacy authorizations (that give those persons named as proxies or agents access to your medical records) are now required under the Health Insurance Portability and Accountability Act (HIPAA.)

The consequences of not having Durable Powers of Attorney and Health Care Directives in place have been made clear in sad cases involving Nancy Cruzan and Terri Schiavo where, for lack of clear guidance, courts had to decide whether they would have chosen to end life support. In addition to battling over what the two women would have decided, the Schiavo case presented wildly different views of her prognosis. The damage to families caught in such circumstances is almost incalculable and the financial cost can be astronomical.

Providing for Your Beneficiaries

Leaving a will is only one of the ways to provide for children or loved ones after you die. Joint accounts avoid the need for a will, since they become the sole property of the surviving owner. Similarly, assets placed into trusts will pass to your beneficiaries without probate (the legal process by which a will is proved to be valid). Insurance policies, annuities and most retirement funds will also automatically go to beneficiaries without the use of a will.

WAYS TO TRANSFER ASSETS ON DEATH

* Will

* Trust

* Designation - 401(k)s, IRAs

* Joint Accounts

* In-Trust-for, Pay-on-Death Accounts

Consulting with an attorney about your estate will help you understand exactly what assets will pass automatically to your heirs and what assets need to be mentioned in a will to pass to those you wish to benefit. Only assets you own in your own name will pass by a will. If you don't leave a will, your assets will automatically be distributed to spouses and blood relatives in proportions predetermined by law. The state's inflexible distribution scheme (intestacy) may clash with what you actually want to happen.

Besides giving you control over who gets what, most wills pay for themselves simply by excusing the Executor (male) or Executrix (female) from posting sureties on their bonds (in essence insuring against the total amount of the assets passing through the will). Such bonds are expensive and must be renewed annually until the estate is completed. No matter how much one may dislike the probate process, it is often much simpler and less expensive than the distribution process without a will.

You should review your estate plan at least every 10 years because both laws and circumstances change. That nephew you wanted to leave valuable stock to may have lost your confidence in his ability to use the money wisely. Or a child who receives Supplemental Security Income (SSI) as compensation for a disability may lose those benefits if she receives money outright from your estate.

Avoiding Abuse, Scams and Exploitation

A famous criminal, when asked why he robbed banks, responded simply, "That's where the money is." In the 21st century, much of America's wealth is in the hands of people over age 50. Bernie Madoff was not the only crook to realize this and to pitch his Ponzi scheme to folks who were building their retirement savings. One of the fastest growing crimes is financially exploiting people as they age.

Abusers come in all disguises, from televised shopping networks (whose best customers appear to be aging hoarders) to roofers, plumbers and others who perform valuable and needed services. These service providers sometimes exaggerate their costs for older consumers, thinking they may pay less attention to detail. And scams can go on for years before children notice how much their parents are spending. MetLife offers tips for preventing such scams.

But most seniors are financially exploited by their children and other relatives who take advantage of confusion, weakness and even guilt to get parents to make substantial gifts, guarantee personal loans or even to pay huge fees for services arranged by a child. Perhaps the most common abuse is when a child convinces a parent to transfer ownership of the family home with the promise that "the house will be yours even if the deed says otherwise."

Some scams within families are carried out by children who misrepresent Medicaid and other laws. To curb some of these crimes, states are far more vigilant than they used to be. Most counties now have a private or administrative agency (sometimes called a "Protective Service Agency") that investigates cases in which physical or financial abuse is alleged. They can determine in far less time than criminal or civil actions whether someone has been cheated. If this is the finding, criminal action may follow and someone may be appointed to take over custodial and financial care of the individual.

Checklist for Legal Life Planning

Here is a quick, 10-question checklist to help you identify how well prepared you are to deal with the legal threats and uncertainties covered in this chapter.

Yes	No	Checklist Questions
		1. Do you know how and when to enroll in the various Medicare options and how to obtain supplemental insurance?
		2. Do you know what your Social Security benefits will be, what option to take and when?
		3.a. Do you have a will and/or trust that you have reviewed and updated in the last 10 years? 3.b. Have you discussed it with the person you have designated as Executor?
		4.a. Have you signed a Durable Power of Attorney that designates someone to handle your financial affairs if you cannot? 4.b. Have you reviewed your financial affairs with that person?
		5.a. Have you signed a Health Care Proxy that identifies someone to make decisions about your health care if you are unable? 5.b. Have you discussed your preferences with that person?

Yes	No	Checklist Questions
		6.a. Have you reviewed your beneficiary designations for IRAs, 401(k)s, insurance policies and other assets in the past 10 years? 6.b. Do your beneficiaries know you have selected them?
		7. Have you set up joint accounts so that the money in those accounts can be transferred directly to a spouse, relative or friend without the need for probate or other court action?
		8. Do you have a Long-Term Care Insurance policy or other plans to pay for the cost of nursing home or other extended care, should you need it?
		9. Do you know how to identify and deal with possible scams, abuses and exploitations?
		10. Do you have a relationship with an attorney who specializes in the items covered by this checklist?

If you answered "Yes" to most or all of these questions, congratulations! We should all be well prepared to deal with legal dangers that life's uncertainties pose. If you were not able to answer "Yes" to most of these questions, you should make it a priority to work on each question with a "No" answer.

None of us knows precisely what scenarios we may face in our futures. By taking the practical steps identified in this chapter, you will know that you have done your best to prepare for those unforeseen events that may affect your health, your finances and the quality of the life you lead. You will also create some peace of mind for having thoughtfully provided your loved ones with the tools they may need and a clear understanding of your wishes when their assistance is needed.

Life Planning Network Chapter Contributors

Bill Brisk, JD, PhD, Elder Law Attorney, Editor-In-Chief of the *National Association of Elder Law Attorneys Journal*, www. briskelderlaw.com. (Chapter Leader)

Resources

Social Security and Medicare

www.ssa.gov/retire2/ — Social Security Retirement Planner helps you determine the various benefit options and the best age to apply for Social Security benefits.

www.ssa.gov/estimator/ — If you have enough Social Security credits to retire, but you are not yet receiving benefits, visit this site to estimate your Social Security retirement benefit.

www.medicare.gov/navigation/medicare-basics/coverage-choices. aspx — The official U.S. Government site for Medicare, *Your Medicare Coverage Choices.*

Long-Term Care and Medicaid

www.longtermcare.gov/LTC/Main_Site/index.aspx — National Clearinghouse for Long-Term Care Information includes information about planning for, financing and understanding long-term care.

https://www.cms.gov/medicaidgeninfo/ — General information about Medicaid. Information about Medicaid for long-term care can be found at www.medicare.gov/LongTermCare/Static/ PayingOverview.asp

www.briskelderlaw.com — For information about post-hospital Medicare coverage, read *Medicare Benefit After 'Plateau.'*

Scams, Abuses and Financial Exploitation

www.ncea.aoa.gov/Main_Site/Find_Help/APS/Analysis_State_ Laws.aspx — National Center on Elder Abuse, *Analysis of State Protective Services Laws.*

www.justice.gov/archive/elderjustice.htm — United States Department of Justice, *Elder Justice.*

http://helpguide.org/mental/elder_abuse_physical_emotional_ sexual_neglect.htm — HelpGuide.org, *Elder Abuse and Neglect.*

www.metlife.com/assets/cao/mmi/publications/studies/2011/ Tips/mmi-preventing-elder-financial-abuse-older-adults. pdf — The MetLife Mature Market Institute has created a list of *Planning Tips* for preventing scams, abuses and exploitation of older people.

Elder Law

www.naela.org — National Academy of Elder Law Attorneys.

Well-Being for Life —
Daily Choices — Creating Lasting Vitality

> *"The difference between the impossible and the possible lies in a person's determination."*
> — *Tommy Lasorda*

JOAN, AN ACCOMPLISHED 53-YEAR-OLD organizational consultant, was enjoying a summer outing with her family and a colleague in 2007, when suddenly her life changed forever. Joan's colleague, who had just recently earned her pilot's license, offered to take Joan's family up for a ride in a rented Piper-Cherokee. The plane only had four seats, so Joan's husband and his excited kids took the first ride. Joan was a little nervous when her turn came for the second ride, but she summoned the nerve and climbed on board.

As the plane took off, Joan realized that her reluctance was about placing her safety in the hands of a novice pilot. But airborne and looking down from the sky, Joan was soon enjoying herself. All was fine until the return landing. The pilot overshot the approach. The engine stalled and the plane dropped 30 feet onto the tarmac. The pilot tried to regain control. She pulled the nose up enough to avoid the trees at the end of the runway, but crashed in a swamp 500 feet away.

Joan doesn't remember the crash or the first two days in the trauma unit. She suffered a total of 14 fractures and a serious head injury resulting in neurological damage. The doctors told her she would never be able to handle complex work again and would be on disability for the rest of her life. "That news was almost as traumatizing as the crash itself," Joan recalls.

In the weeks that followed, Joan endured a roller coaster of physical and emotional highs and lows. She could have resigned herself to the bleak words of her doctors. But she refused to accept their view of the future and, little by little, was able to adopt the attitude that this accident was a life challenge to take charge of and manage. She summoned the inner resources that had served her well in her personal and professional life. She began plugging away on her journey back to "wellness," intent on recovering mobility, total neurological function and living a full life. Four years later, at the age of 57, having made a remarkable comeback, Joan pictures herself working and thriving into her late 70s. "And you need to be healthy to do that," she says.

Wellness requires vision, goal setting, knowledge, planning, determination and effort. It's a cumulative process that develops steadily over a lifetime. Sometimes luck is against you, as in Joan's case, and it may seem that life is out of your hands. But whether or not you encounter adversity in life, breeze through without a hitch or find yourself somewhere in between, mindset and attitude can drive choices that empower you to take charge. Each and every life circumstance, including yours, is unique and offers its own challenges. As you follow Joan's story below, you may discover that her recovery illustrates ways of living smart that you can incorporate into your own life plan.

What Is Your Vision for Yourself?

One of Joan's steps toward wellness was to visualize herself as a fully functioning, healthy woman in her future. How do you visualize yourself as you move through your second half of life?

1. Think of the things that you like to do today and want to continue doing as you get older.

2. Visualize yourself as that older person doing and enjoying these activities.

3. Imagine yourself involved with other activities in your future that you never had time for — starting a new venture, skiing

with friends, traveling with family, playing tennis, continuing to learn and taking courses, enjoying board games on the floor with grandkids.

4. Examine the contribution that your health and wellness play in your vision.

So What is "Wellness" Anyway?

*"If I'd known I was gonna live this long,
I'd have taken better care of myself."*
— Eubie Blake

As Joan overcame the first painfully difficult stages of recovery, she pictured a three-year plan to move herself toward positive health. Her primary challenge was to heal and restore her crushed body. She spent three hours every day doing physical and occupational therapies at Spaulding Rehabilitation Hospital in Boston. Physical therapy continued at her home for three months, then for many more months at the rehab clinic. She found other ways to cope and manage her healing process including a daily meditation practice with support from her yoga teacher and regular massage therapy at her home. Joan states, "I have become stronger in my heart and intuition through this healing process. I am a wiser, more empathic woman and my professional work as a leadership developer has grown stronger too."

No matter what your personal circumstances are, your own path toward wellness is:

1. About choosing to take charge of your life. It is active.

2. A continuing process involving your awareness, education and growth. It has no endpoint.

3. The interplay and relationship between your body, mind, emotion and spirit.

Dr. John W. Travis, the pioneering physician and author who first brought the term "wellness" into public awareness, writes, "Wellness is the right and privilege of everyone. There is no prerequisite for it other than your free choice. The 'well' being is not necessarily the strong, the brave, the successful, the young, the whole, or even the illness-free being. A person can be living a process of wellness and yet be physically handicapped, aged, scared in the face of challenge, in pain, and imperfect. No matter what your current state of health, you can begin to appreciate yourself as a growing, changing person and allow yourself to move toward a happier life and positive health." (www.thewellspring.com)

Iceberg Model of Health and Disease

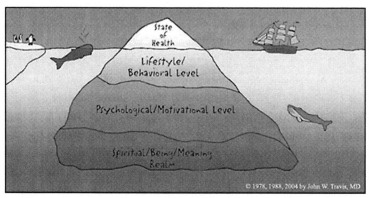

In Dr. Travis's "Iceberg Model of Health and Disease," a person's current state of health is portrayed as the visible tip of the iceberg. It's how you are seen by the rest of the world and it's supported by various dimensions of your inner life below the surface. Understanding, developing and improving these — your physical, mental and emotional health as well as your spiritual life — will improve your "state of health" visible to the rest of the world.

Dr. Travis' Iceberg Model of Health and Disease portrays what he calls your current "state of health," that is what you show to the world, as just the tip of an iceberg created and shored up by your personal supportive levels under the surface. Understanding, developing and improving the levels below the surface, including your physical, mental and emotional health, plus your spirituality, will improve the "state of your health" visible above the surface.

How Will You Reach Your Vision?

Joan spent the years after the crash developing and implementing a wellness plan to heal her body and move toward her vision of being a fully functioning, healthy woman. What are some steps that would help you reach your vision for yourself?

1. Explore the different levels in the Iceberg Model by studying the descriptions on the Wellspring website. *

2. Pick two levels from the Iceberg Model that you could work on to help you attain your vision.

3. Make a list of three action steps to address each of those areas.

4. Create a "self care" plan implementing at least one action step from each area this week. Continue to develop and implement more action steps next week and beyond.

5. Expand and develop your list after you finish exploring and learning from this chapter.

---

* www.thewellspring.com/wellspring/introduction-to-wellness/359/
key-concept-2-the-iceberg-model-of-health-and-disease.cfm

Physical Health — What Do Lifestyle and Behavior Have to Do with Physical Aging?

"Years may wrinkle the skin, but to
give up enthusiasm wrinkles the soul."
— *Samuel Ullman*

Three years after the crash, Joan started physical training at the gym. Her broken bones were mended but her body wasn't healed. Her body was shut down and guarded with stiffness and a restriction of movement. Her posture was slumped and her neck was practically rigid as if she was afraid to move. She still had significant pain in her back and her muscles were terribly de-conditioned. Despite all this, she was ready to explore this next step and get to work. "The biggest obstacle to recovery is how you see yourself in the future," she says. At 53, the game's not over.

The goal at first was to gently get Joan's body to open up and start to move again. More time and patience was needed to heal her connective tissues, restore her posture and regain her confidence in her physical body.

Although more extreme, Joan's closed and stiffened condition brings to mind the physical state of many people in the second half of life. Strain from habitually closed posture, poor breathing habits, stress, harmful movement patterns and aging can cause connective tissues in your body to thicken and stiffen. This restrictive condition worsens over time if you sit too long at the computer or watching TV, exercise too little or too much, or are unaware of your body positioning and emotional challenges. In Joan's case, it was the result of having her body crushed and mangled in a plane crash.

Stiffened connective tissues restrict movement and often can cause you pain. Pain creates movement compensations that can create new patterns of strain and more pain. It's a vicious cycle. Pete Egoscue, author of *Pain Free, A Revolutionary Method for Stopping Chronic Pain*, writes: "By rediscovering the body's design and allowing it to work as intended, many of the disabling conditions that take such a financial and personal toll can be reversed or avoided altogether. Motion is absolutely crucial to the body's operations and overall welfare."

Mary Bond, a structural integration practitioner, tells us there is a strong "relationship between your posture, your pain, your habits of movement, and your aging process." In her book, *The New Rules of Posture: How to Sit, Stand, and Move in the Modern World,* she says, "When bodies are stiff and movement is restricted people look and feel old." She wisely advises that, "Aging happens to us all. Knowing how to use your body well will make a huge difference in how you experience the process."

Breathing well and aging well are also related. Cultivating a habit of deep, smooth and rhythmic breathing has been shown to positively influence your heart rate, blood pressure, circulation and digestion. Dr. Andrew Weil, perhaps one of the most influential physician-writers of the alternative and complementary medicine movement, says, "If I had to limit my advice on healthier living to just one tip, it would be simply to learn how to breathe correctly."*

The importance of healthy connective tissue, good posture, proper movement patterns and breathing habits is often overlooked. They are all strongly related to how you feel physically and emotionally about yourself as you age.

Also, being knowledgeable about the differences between real physical aging and deterioration from life events and lifestyle habits can help you age well too. *Many diseases of aging are really diseases of lifestyle and behavioral choices.* Your own choices about nutrition, physical activity, smoking, alcohol and drug use (including prescription drugs), relationships with friends and family and how you manage stress, among other things, can make you biologically older than your chronological years, or conversely, keep you younger and more vital than you might imagine.

As part of a population that is already navigating the second half of life, you want to be well *and* to be well for as long as possible. To lead a long healthy life, to age well, is a continuous process that involves

---

* www.drweil.com/drw/u/ART00521/three-breathing-exercises.html

your choice to be an active participant. There is that powerful and optimistic word again – CHOICE. You can take control. You can be in charge. A lot of this wellness stuff really is up to you. Just ask Joan.

You Can Easily Improve Two Important Lifestyle Habits Through Awareness

Your Posture

Joan paid attention to reestablishing good postural alignment during her healing process. Many people never notice their posture until the cumulative effects of gravity make poor postural habits a problem, including chronic neck pain, headaches and balance issues. Awareness is the first step toward improvement.

1. Take a look in a full-length mirror. Notice your shoulder position. Are you rounded forward?

2. Look sideways in the mirror and check out your upper back and head position. Is your chest slumped and head forward?

3. Sit on the edge of a chair with your feet and knees hip width apart, maintain a chin tuck, raise your chest up allowing your spine to relax into a gentle arch. Relax your shoulders, then rotate your shoulders, arms and hands backward and down. Hold the position for 10 breaths, release and repeat throughout your day. This is called the Brugger Relief Position.*

Your Breathing

Many people are shallow breathers, unaware that at times during the day, breathing simply stops. Holding your breath is an automatic response to stress that creates a chronic state of mild hyperventilation, decreasing energy and placing a strain on the heart.

1. Take time throughout the day to check in on your breathing.

---

* www.youtube.com/watch?v=Lgm3j66fpBA

2. Are you holding your breath?

3. What's the quality of your breath? Shallow and constricted or deep and easy flowing? Take breath breaks, breathing deeply into the lower abdomen several times per day as a key way to reduce stress, improve overall health and increase energy.

Mental Health — What Do Attitude and Exercise Have to Do with Longevity and the Brain?

"The last of the human freedoms is to choose one's attitude in any given set of circumstances."
–Victor Frankl

Seven months after the accident, Joan was told that she had three hemorrhages in her brain that might account for her awkward speech hesitation. Months later, she saw a behavioral neurologist at Beth Israel Hospital in Boston who told her that a new MRI of her brain showed that the bleeds were gone and were likely not still causing her speech problems. "What people believe has a great impact on recovery," he said. That notion resonated with Joan as her mindfulness and positive attitude had been a driving force in her recovery. "Within days of hearing that, my speech hesitation was gone," she says.

This might come as little surprise to Ellen Langer*, a Harvard University social psychologist and the author of *Counterclockwise: Mindful Health and the Power of Possibility.* In it, she describes an uncanny experiment she and her graduate students undertook in 1979 to look at what effects turning back the clock psychologically would have on people's physical state. Langer took a group of men in their later seventies and early 80s on a kind of retreat held at an old monastery. The monastery was retrofit to "replicate" the world

---

* Ellen Langer at www.ellenlanger.com/about/

twenty years earlier. All magazines, books, and music were from 1959. The volunteers agreed to hold all conversations as if it were currently 1959, including discussions about themselves, politics, sports, or the world. At the end of the week, on many measures the men appeared to be "younger." On intelligence tests, 63 percent improved their scores. Joint flexibility and dexterity improved and measurements of fingers showed lengthening. There were also improvements of height, weight, gait, and posture resulting in a younger appearance. Men who could barely shuffle off the bus when they arrived were playing touch football with Langer by the time they left.

Langer writes about the transformative effects of embracing the psychology of possibility, which "first requires that we begin with the assumption that we do not know what we can do or become," and second, that we "try out different things without evaluating ourselves as we go along." Her research, which has continued over the thirty years since that initial experiment, suggests that if we open our minds to what is possible rather than remain stuck in precepts of impossibility, we will be better stewards of our own health.

Jon Kabat-Zinn is the founder and former director of the stress reduction program at the University of Massachusetts Medical Center. His life work has been to bring awareness of the benefits of the mainstream of medicine and society. "When we use the word healing to describe the experiences of people in the stress clinic, what we mean above all is that they are undergoing a profound transformation of view," Kabat-Zinn writes in his book, *Full Catastrophe Living*. "Out of this shift in perspective comes an ability to act with greater balance and inner security in the world."

The "profound transformation of view" that Kabat-Zinn speaks of can be associated with one's personal approach to attitude. It's widely accepted that leading a physically active life contributes to longevity, but research suggests that positive attitude is associated with better health, wellness and longevity as well. Lending credence to that theory is a study conducted by psychologist Becca Levy at Yale University in the late 1990s. It found people with positive views on aging lived an average of 7.6 years longer than those with negative views.

By the third year of Joan's recovery she was physically strong enough to intensify her cardiovascular training in the gym. That was great news for her brain. Exercise creates stronger connections between brain cells and stimulates formation of new ones. Exercise supplies and nourishes your brain with oxygen. It elevates your mood and boosts motivation. It can combat the biological effects of too much stress. It boosts immune function, reduces obesity and regulates fuel metabolism.

According to Dr. John Ratey, author of *Spark: The Revolutionary New Science of Exercise and the Brain,* starting at about age 40 we lose on average five percent of our overall brain volume per decade up until about age seventy. Exercise slows the process. It fosters neuroplasticity in the brain so you can actually grow new brain cells. Says Ratey, "Exercise prepares neurons to connect, while mental stimulation, learning and an enriched environment allow your brain to capitalize on that readiness."

It is known that the main causes of "diseases of aging" are inactivity, poor eating habits and smoking. The same things that kill the body, kill the brain. Ratey asserts that many of the same factors that can reduce our risk for cardiovascular disease and diabetes also reduce the risk for age-related neurodegenerative disorders.

Mindful behavior, positive attitude and exercise are essential catalysts for developing your mental health. Brain function can benefit even from modest amounts of exercise. And since exercise can elevate your mood, it's natural to think it can also affect your attitude and outlook on life in a positive way.

Develop an Exercise Program to Keep Your Brain Sharp

Develop some exercise strategies that you can regularly weave into your everyday life. Take a brisk walk to elevate your heart rate, take every opportunity to use the stairs, sweep the floor, cut the grass, wash the windows, take a class at the gym and hire a personal trainer. These are terrific ways to get you moving more often. During exercise, think about the way that you move your posture and breathing patterns. Remember, it will take time for your body to adjust to any new physical demands that you place on it. Be consistent and persistent, increase your activity level a little at a time and stay with it to see results. You may need to seek professional guidance to prevent injury if you're currently a sedentary individual, have orthopedic issues or cardiac risks. Please be sure to consult your doctor first if you have risk factors.

Emotional Health — What Does Forgiveness Have to Do with Wellness and Inner Peace?

"The moment when you understand, compassion is born in your heart. And now it is possible for you to forgive … not before that."
—*Thich Nhat Hanh*

When Joan first woke up in the hospital, she told her husband that she was totally responsible for the situation in which she found herself. It was her decision to get into the airplane in the first place. As time trudged on, though, it became clear to her that rather than being angry with herself, her main issue was going to be one of forgiving her colleague, the pilot. Joan went through a year of psychotherapy, attended seminars on forgiveness, read books on the topic and gave herself two years before finally talking to the pilot. Joan laments, "I couldn't rush it. It took time for me. It was a process."

Forgiving those who have caused personal harm is a critical component of achieving emotional health. However, emotional health encompasses a vast range of issues including depression, anxiety, addiction and other conditions, all of which may impact your physical health too. Being emotionally healthy also means managing day-to-day issues like stress, changing bad habits, making and keeping friendships (see our chapter on "The Relationship Dividend") and using creativity (see our chapter on "Awaken Your Creativity"), many of which Joan had to wrestle with. Finding forgiveness, though, was by far one of her biggest challenges.

Forgiveness is not condoning or forgetting, but a means of coming to inner peace and seeing the core humanity of all people. It's not just an intellectual exercise either. Experiencing a grievance is a mind-body disturbance, and arriving at inner peace can be a challenging process that requires your patience and emotional bravery. First, it requires finding a way to "be" with difficult emotions and thoughts, e.g. anger, resentment and desire for revenge. Then ways must be discovered to release the victim stance at all levels — mind, body and spirit. Forgiveness is a choice that ultimately unhooks you from the past and allows you to live more fully in the present moment, without the victim narrative being central to your personal identity.

Researchers at the University of Wisconsin-Madison are dedicated to helping people gain knowledge about forgiveness and to use that knowledge for personal, group, and societal renewal. Professor Robert Enright speaks of a stage called "seeing with new eyes," as the forgiver sees that the "injuring person is more than the offenses she has committed. The forgiver sees the unconditional worth of the other as a person, which can lead to empathy and compassion and eventually to the willingness to offer goodness to the other out of mercy. It is here that forgiveness takes root, opening up the possibility of restored emotional and relational health."

Multiple studies have shown that people can not only learn forgiveness but that those who forgive are happier, healthier, more compassionate, vital, optimistic, self-confident, and experience less stress.

Will Forgiveness Help You to Reach Your Vision?

Joan knew that harboring anger toward her colleague would prevent her from moving forward. Inevitably, forgiveness was the way to overcome this obstacle in her wellness process.

1. Think of one person who has been a challenge in your life — someone who created difficulty for you, frustrated you, hurt you, or with whom you have argued.

2. Identify five admirable qualities about that person.

3. Find common qualities between you that indicate you might be alike in some ways.

4. Remember those similarities the next time you are around that

person.

5. Put yourself in the other person's shoes to understand both sides of the story.

6. Realize the unconditional worth of the person.

7. Develop empathy and compassion toward that person and then lead yourself to forgiveness.

"Aging Well" Requires Multiple Strategies of "Living Smart"

When you think about it, Joan's process toward wellness reflects many strategies that could be used to successfully navigate the second half of life. As with Joan, every person has their own life challenges including the challenges of aging. You, for example, may feel great and notice only subtle, insignificant changes as you become older. Or you may notice that you are feeling stiff, old and creaky. Pain may be something you live with every day. Your medical measures may be starting to change. You might feel depressed, isolated or without support. Regrets about things that could have been, or worries about events that are coming disturb your psyche. Those "senior moments" may occur a little more frequently.

It may seem like it happened overnight, but the aging process started back in your third decade of life. In more youthful days, perhaps you had the intuition or foresight to develop strategies and practices to set the stage for optimal health and wellness in the second half of your life. However, many times people wait until a significant decline in health or the occurrence of a catastrophic event before tuning in to answer the wakeup call. Staying well then becomes reactive rather than proactive.

What are some of the lessons you can learn from Joan's story? What is your mindset and attitude about living smart? Do you have a proactive, evolving plan to realize the vision that you created for your second half of life from earlier in the chapter? Are you learning, expanding your awareness and growing? Are you in charge of your wellness process? The good news is that the human body is marvelously resilient. It is never too late to explore, develop and exercise multiple "taking care" practices just like Joan.

Today, Joan has resumed her position as a high-level international management consultant. Her amazing determination and belief in herself have paid off. She continues to travel around the world, facilitate team meetings, write articles and teach graduate students at Boston University's School of Public Health. As she continues her life process to be a "well being" she is excited and optimistic about what's coming tomorrow, and in the years to come. Recently, Joan attended her 35th college reunion and had an epiphany. "It occurred to me that if I stay healthy, I could have as many more productive, contributing years going forward as I have had from college to this very day."

And that's a lot of years left to go. Just ask Joan.

Life Planning Network Chapter Contributors

Moira Lanier, Founder, President and Master Trainer, Greatest Age Fitness, Inc., www.greatestagefitness.com. (Chapter Leader)

Barbara Abramowitz, M Ed, LMHC, LMFT, Licensed Psychotherapist and Certified Body-Mind Life Coaching™ Specialist, www.optimallivingnow.com.

Resources

Exercise and Nutrition

J.E. Anderson and S. Prior, "Nutrition and Aging," Colorado State University, www.ext.colostate.edu/pubs/foodnut/09322.html#top

Mary Bond, *The New Rules of Posture: How to Sit, Stand, and Move in the Modern World*, Healing Arts Press, 2006.

Jane Fonda, *Prime Time: Love, Health, Sex, Fitness, Friendship, Spirit — Making the Most of All of Your Life*, Random House, 2011.

Jane Fonda, "Working Out," *Health and Fitness*, September 19, 2011.

Thomas Meyers, "Massage," Anatomy Trains, www.anatomytrains.com.

John Ratey, MD, Spark: *The Revolutionary New Science of Exercise and the Brain*, Little, Brown and Company, 2008.

Aging

Muriel Gillick, MD, *The Denial of Aging: Perpetual Youth, Eternal Life, and Other Dangerous Fantasies*, Harvard University Press, 2007.

Scott McCredie, *Balance: In Search of the Lost Sense*, Little, Brown and Company, 2007.

Maryan Pelland, "How Age Changes Your Body," Suite101, 2006.

Camille Peri, "Talking with Becca Levy: Age Stereotypes and Elder Health," Caring.com. <www.caring.com/interviews >

Andrew Weil, MD, *Healthy Aging: A Lifelong Guide to Your Well-Being*, Anchor, 2007.

Mental Health

Edmunds J. Bourne, *The Anxiety and Phobia Workbook*, New Harbinger Publications, 2011.

The Dalai Lama and Howard C. Cutler, *The Art of Happiness, a Handbook for Living*, Riverhead Books, 1998.

Martin Doblmeier, "The Power of Forgiveness," Journey Films, 2008.

Robert Enright, PhD, "Why Forgive?," International Forgiveness Institute.

Robert Enright, PhD and Roy Lloyd, "The Science of Forgiveness," Huffington Post, June 16, 2010.

Mark Williams, John Teasdale, Zindel Segal & Jon Kabat-Zinn, *The Mindful Way Through Depression: Freeing Yourself from Chronic Unhappiness*, Guilford, 2007.

Lea Winerman, "A Healthy Mind, a Longer Life." The APA Monitor, 37, 10. 2006. <www.apa.org/monitor/nov06/healthy.aspx>.

Lifestyle Change

James O. Prochaska, PhD, *Changing for Good, A Revolutionary Six-Stage Program for Overcoming Bad Habits and Moving your Life Positively Forward*, Harper Paperbacks, 1995.

"The Key to Making Lasting Lifestyle and Behavioral Changes: Is It Will or Skill?" American Psychological Association Help Center.

Ellen Langer, PhD, *Counterclockwise, Mindful Health and the Power of Possibility*, Ballantine Books, 2009.

John Travis, "Key Concept #2: The Iceberg Model of Health and Disease," TheWellspring www.thewellspring.com/.

Pain and Stress

Pete Egoscue, *Pain Free, A Revolutionary Method for Stopping Chronic Pain*, Bantam, 2000.

Pete Egoscue, "What is Egoscue?," Egoscue.com.

Robert M. Sapolsky, *Why Zebras Don't Get Ulcers, The Acclaimed Guide to Stress, Stress-Related Diseases, and Coping*, Holt Paperbacks, 2004.

Jon Kabat-Zinn, PhD, *Full Catastrophe Living: Using the Wisdom of Your Body and Mind to Face Stress, Pain, and Illness*, Delta, 1990.

Without Delay —
Anticipating Caregiving Challenges

LIFE WAS GOOD FOR TERESA, a 63-year-old California health care professional, and Ed, her husband of 43 years. That is, until she slipped and fell down the stairs while visiting her daughter and grandchildren. She sustained a traumatic brain injury and, after six weeks in a hospital and two months in rehab, she returned to her home.

Her home ... not her life.

In an instant, life had changed. The couple's imagined future — with Teresa working a few more years to save for a comfortable retirement and spending time as involved grandparents — had evaporated. The brain injury from the accident left Teresa depressed, erratic, irrational, jealous and unemployable. Disability payments arrived from Social Security, but they didn't cover her expenses as her salary had. Because she now suffered poor judgment, mood swings and the inability to plan, Ed took over all meal preparation, bill paying, planning and more. He, like many caregivers, lost his lifelong partner and had to assume roles he never imagined would be his.

The couple had written a will, but they had done little else that might have helped prepare for what unfolded. They had no health directives, no trusts, no long-term health insurance. And they had not wrestled with the giant "what if" of caregiving.

"Unfortunately, we didn't think we needed those things yet," said Ed.

Denial, delay, distractions and delusion are but a few of the ways we avoid dealing with the high probability that we will need care from others or find ourselves providing it.

Former First Lady Rosalynn Carter, who heads the Rosalynn Carter Institute for Caregiving, told a U.S. Senate Special Committee on

Aging: "There are only four kinds of people in the world — those who have been caregivers, those who are currently caregivers, those who will be caregivers and those who will need caregivers."

As life planners, we'd like to help you break through the barrier of this often taboo subject. Proper planning can help you to live smart — it can clarify choices, reduce risks and expand options. We'll suggest steps to help you avoid the consequences of not planning from both perspectives — as someone needing care and as someone providing it. We start with receiving care, because if you've faced your own possible future caregiving needs, you'll be better equipped to deal with those of your loved ones, which the bulk of the chapter addresses.

When You Need Care

Whether due to a fall, a chronic disease like diabetes or Alzheimer's, limited mobility or advancing frailty ... whether sudden or long progressing ... thanks to increasing longevity, most of us are virtually guaranteed to eventually require some kind of *long-term* care.

Still, even those who plan seriously for retirement commonly retreat from budgeting for unforeseen health care costs and wrestling with the critical questions of who will provide caregiving and how to pay for it. We (and that includes even the professionals who advise others) blindly accept the significant risk of doing nothing.

But inaction does nothing to alter inevitability.

Some 21 million Americans required long-term care in 2008. About 70 percent of all people over the age of 65 will require some long-term care services during their lifetime.

While not oblivious to these unhappy probabilities, most make only the sketchiest plans. Like Teresa and Ed, we likely see a lawyer and prepare a will. Maybe we have a power of attorney and an advanced health care directive drawn, in case bad luck like theirs incapacitates us. That's all good. Readying such basic legal documents is important.

But it's hardly enough. Without more conscious, active planning to anticipate our caregiving needs, dreams cherished for the second half of life may dissolve in an instant and be replaced by costly caregiving nightmares. Sometimes we address the issues in the nick of time. Far too often, we attend to them too late.

Ask yourself:

- ▓ Who will take care of me? For how long? Have I discussed this with the person I am counting on for help? Do I have a backup plan?

- ▓ How will I pay for care? Do I qualify for state or federal subsidies?

- ▓ Where do I want to live if I need long-term care? What are my living options if I need more care than I can get in my home?

After we ask these basic questions, we might consider how few real answers we have and just how frightening — and well founded — is our uncertainty. After all, we'd never start a business without developing a business plan.

Why, then, are we willing to leave to chance our care in the event of disabling illness or incremental decline? Why — even though doing so would save time, money and stress for our caregivers and help guide them to meet our needs — are we reluctant to discuss and delegate the tasks, resources, responsibilities and contingencies that could come into play? How, then, should we plan?

Taking Control:

You might best begin by imagining all plausible scenarios for needing caregiving. Then envision your needs and how you want to be cared for. Identify the person you'd like to assume primary responsibility for your care. Early on, consult with a lawyer competent in elder law to prepare a will, a health directive, power of attorney, and a trust (if necessary). Review Medicare, health insurance, and, if you have it, long-term care insurance policies and get informed about your benefits. (Also see the chapter on "Your Wishes Matter.")

Once you've taken those steps, initiate a conversation with family members or loved ones to establish your plan. Hold a formal meeting. Doing so will help underscore the significance of what you are doing and break down resistance others might have about addressing the subject. Designate a personal care coordinator (and a backup) who will make sure your plan is implemented. Provide a checklist for finances, legal documents and their locations, and medical care. Be candid, clear and comprehensive. It will help you attain your goals for care and reduce the burden and guilt caregivers might feel.

Ideally, caregiving happens at home, where we can continue to lead active lives, socialize with friends and family, and stay connected to sources of personal happiness. So, it's crucial to manage your environment proactively to protect your health. To avoid the risk of falls and other issues, assess the renovations that may be needed. Will entrances need to be made accessible? Are bedrooms and bathrooms on the first floor? Will light switches need to be lowered? At what cost? Consider consulting with a certified aging-in-place specialist to put together a complete plan.

Sometimes the unexpected may make our plans for aging in place difficult or no longer feasible. In case our abilities decline and it becomes necessary, it's also important to investigate options that provide moderate assistance, including local support services, co-housing communities, Naturally Occurring Retirement Communities (NORCs), assisted living facilities, continuing care retirement communities, as well as nursing homes for when more serious assistance is needed.

When It's You Providing the Care

When the role of caregiving arrives on our doorsteps, we may hope its visit is brief. It may be, at first. But too often caregiving moves in full time. It takes over our homes, our bank accounts, our relationships and our time from each and every day.

If you don't believe it, just ask some of the 44 million Americans providing 37 billion hours of unpaid, "informal" care each year to family members and friends. Ask them, too, about the staggering costs. Working Americans lose an estimated $3 trillion per year in wages, pensions and Social Security benefits for time they need to take off to provide care for their aging parents, according to a 2011 MetLife study, produced in conjunction with the National Alliance for Caregiving and the Center for Long-Term Care Research Policy at New York Medical College.

Family caregivers expend an average of $5,531 per year. Put another way, women, on average, lose $324,044 of lifetime income, while men lose $283,716, when they become caregivers, according to the study.

What's more, the percentage of adults providing care to a parent — 17 percent of men and 28 percent of women — has more than tripled since 1994. And as life expectancy (now 78 years) continues to rise, the majority of people over 50 today will eventually die of chronic rather than acute illness. In other words, family members will be even more taxed to provide care than they are now.

Facing the issues

Caregiving can be a richly rewarding experience. It can provide a profound sense of purpose and meaning. It can allow a unique opportunity for intimacy and giving that we may have missed in living the hurly burly of our busy lives. However, as an unplanned necessity in which we substitute improvisation for planning, out-of-pocket costs for needed income, burnout and resentment for generosity and loving kindness, caregiving can wreak havoc on our lives. Also, when we have to act in crisis, we focus on immediate decisions and often fail to see the big picture. That can lead us to make choices that are neither our best nor wisest.

Ask yourself:

- Is the recipient ready to accept my caregiving? Have we discussed it together?

- How will I take time off from work to give care? How much?

- Can I get paid for caring for a family member?

Honest appraisal is as critical as courage. Each situation may have slightly different answers, but avoiding questions and leaving answers in limbo until crisis makes them inescapable is to no one's advantage. Lack of shared information can as easily pave the way to a disappointed care recipient as to a caregiver who incrementally accumulates a burdensome list of responsibilities. Then, in an eye blink, the situation mushrooms and we end up asking, "How'd I become a full-time caregiver with no help, no time, no life?"

As Connie Goldman writes in *The Gifts of Caregiving,* "We take on the role of the caregiver because the alternatives aren't acceptable to our families or ourselves. Often we don't know what we're getting into, but we make the leap anyway, take on the responsibility and hope for the best."

The average caregiver is a 49-year-old, married, employed woman caring for her widowed 69-year-old mother, according to the National Alliance for Caregiving in collaboration with AARP (2009). The caregiver assumes her role modestly at first. She does a little shopping. She brings an occasional meal. She takes her mother to medical appointments. As her mother's needs increase, the caregiver juggles her work schedule and her roles. She spends more time at work on the phone making caregiving arrangements. She becomes more distracted and less productive. Then her mother is diagnosed with a disabling condition. Unprepared and overwhelmed, she quits her job to take care of her mother and hold things together in her own household.

Ask yourself:

- What would I do in this situation? What are the alternatives?

- Am I prepared to make a major adjustment to my life?

- What are the long-term consequences of quitting work at my age?

- How will I resolve conflicts between needs and preferences of family members?

- How will I handle extreme stress?

When crisis comes, most caregivers aren't able to analyze objectively the emotional, financial and long-term consequences of their decisions. What may look heroic at first may be self-destructive in the long run. The best strategy is to begin asking questions and engage your loved ones in important conversations — NOW.

Taking Positive Steps

If you fear how others (an older parent, a partner) will react, broach the subject of caregiving gingerly. Explain that, at some point, they may need to make long-term decisions on the kind of care they want. But you, as caregiver, may have to make decisions for them if they haven't spelled things out before care is needed. As difficult as it may be for them to relinquish privacy and face uncomfortable possibilities, a discussion can allow all to have their say. Thrashing out issues now will save anguish down the road. The time might come when loved ones can no longer speak for themselves. You'll be grateful then to know how to best honor their wishes. Propose the conversation as a precaution, a loving gift of anticipation.

You don't need to resolve everything at once. But beginning the conversation is critical.

As you explore becoming a caregiver, ask yourself:

- How will caregiving affect my personal and professional life?
- How will I stay involved in interests and activities that are important to me?
- What are my options for a more flexible work schedule or time off from work?
- What benefits does my state or employer offer for caregivers?
- How will I manage financially if I must cut back on my work hours or need to contribute financially towards my loved one's care?
- Will doing so affect my own health insurance and retirement?
- Is it in everyone's best interest for me to become the caregiver?

Getting the right information and help

If you think you may become the caregiver to your loved one or if you've already assumed the caregiver role, start gathering current, accurate, appropriate and specific information. It may be helpful to have a social worker, geriatric care manager or representative of a local service agency conduct a professional assessment of your loved one's needs to help develop a long-term plan. Usually, this includes an accounting of the care receiver's medical, physical, financial, social, psychological and spiritual needs as well as the medical, financial, social and psychological impact on the caregiver. Assessment services are not covered by insurance, but getting help to navigate the intimidating maze of issues is well worth the expense.

The National Association of Area Agencies on Aging and 1-800-AGE-INFO will both refer you to local resources for seniors and those with disabilities. Some may offer assessment services as well. You can also access information on the Internet from the U.S.

Department of Health and Human Services "Eldercare Locator" program.

Photograph used with permission from Family Caregiver Alliance

Being a caregiver is never an easy responsibility, but having reliable information – whether about pertinent medical conditions or government programs such as Medicare – can reduce the stress that often compounds its challenges. It's important to seek out disease-specific information, especially when caregiving for a loved one with dementia. Remember, the best ways to respond may not be intuitive. Disease-specific organizations, such as the Alzheimer's Association, the American Parkinson's Disease Association, and the American Heart Association, are set up to help people with diseases and provide support and resources to caregivers.

Taking care of yourself as a caregiver

As a caregiver, you face serious challenges of your own. Self-care is, therefore, vitally important. Why? Here are a few clarifying facts:

The duration of caregiving can last from less than a year to more than 40 years. The average is 4.3 years, according to a study by the National Alliance for Caregiving and AARP. Fifty percent of those surveyed spent less than eight hours a week on caregiving, while it consumed more than 40 hours a week for 20 percent of all caregivers. For those caring for someone with a cognitive impairment, the average was 84 hours a week.

As a result, the physical and emotional health of caregivers is often compromised. In particular, risk increases for depression, reduced immune response, poor physical health and chronic conditions. Caregivers experience higher levels of stress, anxiety, exhaustion and frustration, and feel guilty about having those responses. They neglect their own health and social needs, make accommodations at work to deal with their caring responsibilities, and lose time with friends and family. Caregivers have higher than average death rates, even up to five to seven years after their duties end.

For more than a decade Paula K. Solomon, MSSW, a life coach who works with caregivers, helped her mother in her struggle with Parkinson's disease. Paula knows "what it's like to hit a wall as a long-term caregiver — to be so exhausted that it's nearly impossible to be patient, to long for some respite between crises, and to feel as if I couldn't go on doing all that I was doing." Luckily, her mother worried about the toll on Paula's life. Her mother would say, "If something happens to you, I'm in big trouble," and encouraged Paula to take time for herself. Paula learned that by following this advice, she was able to care for and *be with* her mother more *wholeheartedly*.

Relentless tasks and perpetual worry can easily consume caregivers who don't have support and occasional relief. A few hours of respite a week may suffice for you. Or you may need a real vacation periodically to replenish your energy and emotions. Without support and respite, caregivers burn out and can't properly care for loved ones. Their own well-being may be jeopardized, undermining both caregiver and care receiver.

Leeza Gibbons, dubbed "the voice of the caregiver" by AARP, knows about the guilt, loneliness and stress of caring for a sick or failing loved one. Inspired by her mother Jean's struggle with Alzheimer's disease, she conceived Leeza's Place, which provides free services for patients and caregivers dealing with chronic illness in eight locations nationwide. "Nobody's a natural-born Mother Teresa or Florence Nightingale all the time. I know I wasn't," says the former *Entertainment Tonight* and *Extra* host and the author of a memoir, *Take Your Oxygen First: Caring for Yourself while Caring for Someone with Memory Loss.*

Caregiving "can feel like a daily test of your patience, strength and will," says Gibbons. She recently revealed her own "caregiver confessions," along with uplifting practical advice on dealing with 12 common caregiving issues for Caring.com, a leading website for caregivers. "You are not alone," she says.

Don't carry on in isolation. Many organizations focus their services on the caregiver, offering information (e.g. "Taking Care of You" from the Family Caregiver Alliance), and support groups that can help. In addition to the support of a friend or a group, consider whether the services of a psychotherapist or a life coach might help you deal with the personal and emotional challenges.

In it for the long term

Long-term care is hands-on help with fundamental daily activities, such as bathing, eating, dressing, transferring and toileting, over a substantial period of time, or assistance needed because of severe cognitive impairment resulting from Alzheimer's disease and other neurological disorders. Beyond this physical care, many elders need additional assistance with life management tasks such as bill paying, shopping or cooking. Most people (83 percent) with long-term care needs live in their own homes. Of those, 78 percent do not hire help, making family critical in providing long-term care.

Ask yourself:
- What changes would enable my loved one to continue to live at home if she/he had physical or cognitive limitations? What would home renovations cost?

- What's the cost of hiring personal care and household assistance for long-term care?

People often have unrealistic views of costs. Investigate which expenses health insurance covers, and which it doesn't. Explore long-term care (LTC) insurance as a viable option, particularly if your loved ones have savings or an estate they hope to protect. LTC insurance may be best purchased in your 50s, when it will be less expensive. It's costly, poses some risks, and may not be right for everyone. Importantly, it provides coverage for services that Medicare, Medicaid and other insurances don't, including services at home, in nursing homes and assisted living.

Planning — Protection for Better Living

Whether as a care receiver or a caregiver, imagining our or our loved one's lives and occupations altered by decline or disease is not a pleasant pastime. But accurately assessing our wishes, situations, support systems, finances and insurance may be among the most important tasks we can undertake for the future. Candid conversation with those we love, in which we let go of the fantasy that we'll remain forever strong and healthy, may help us to preserve dreams and assets and the relationships we most value in this life. We may not have control over the future, but we can at least strive to create a way of caregiving that won't sap us or those who love us of the health, energy, compassion and dignity that we would never want to have taken from others or forfeit for ourselves. Planning protects and is a powerful expression of love.

Life Planning Network Chapter Contributors

Donna Schempp, LCSW, Family Caregiver Alliance, Consultant, dschempp@att.net.

Paula K. Solomon, MSSW, Life Coach specializing in life transitions and helping caregivers maintain well-being, www.TheSeasonsofYourLife.com.

Bruce Frankel, Author of *What Should I Do With the Rest of My Life? True Stories of Finding Success, Passion and New Meaning in the Second Half of Life*, www.brucefrankel.net.

Resources

General

Connie Goldman, *The Gifts of Caregiving: Stories of Hardship, Hope and Healing.* Fairview Press, 2002.

Thomas Graboys, *Life in the Balance: A Physician's Memoir of Life, Love, and Loss with Parkinson's Disease and Dementia.* Union Square Press, 2008.

Gail Sheehy, *Passages in Caregiving: Turning Chaos into Confidence.* Harper Paperbacks, 2011.

Rosalynn Carter Institute for Caregiving, www.rosalynncarter.org/

Planning

James Gambone, PhD, and Rhonda Travland. *Who Says Men Don't Care? A Man's Guide to Balanced and Guilt-Free Caregiving.* Penguin, 2011.

Joseph Matthews, *Long-Term Care: How to Plan & Pay for It,* NOLO, 2010.

Virginia Morris and Robert M. Butler, *How to Care for Aging Parents.* Workman Publishing Company, 2004.

AARP, www.aarp.org/relationships/caregiving-resource-center.

Benefits Check-Up, a free online service that describes the federal and state programs available for people with low income/assets, www.benefitscheckup.org.

Medicare, www.medicare.gov.

National Academy of Elder Law Attorneys, www.naela.org.

National Association of Professional Geriatric Care Managers, www.caremanager.org.

Compassion and Choices, www.compassionandchoices.org.

The National Hospice and Palliative Care Organization, www.nhpco.org.

Caregiver Support

Children of Aging Parents (CAPS), www.caps4caregivers.org.

Eldercare Locator, www.eldercare.gov.

Family Caregiver Alliance, www.caregiver.org.

Viki Kind, *The Caregiver's Path to Compassionate Decision Making: Making Choices for Those Who Can't,* Greenleaf Book Group Press, 2010.

National Alliance for Caregiving, www.caregiving.org.

The National Association of Area Agencies on Aging, www.n4a.org.

Well Spouse Foundation, www.wellspouse.org.

Terra Nova Films, Inc., *VideoCaregiving,* www.videocaregiving.org.

1-800-AGE-INFO, www.ageinfo.com.

Organizing Caregiving Services

Lotsa Helping Hands, www.lotsahelpinghands.com.

Share the Care, www.sharethecare.org.

Tyze, www.tyze.com.

The Right Place —
Creating a home for your changing needs

THE TRANSITION TO THE SECOND HALF of life prompts pressing questions.

"As we begin addressing these questions, some people experience subtle, and then profound, changes in their feeling about home or in their connection to possessions."

— *Clare Cooper Marcus*, House as a Mirror of Self:
Exploring the Deeper Meaning of Home

Ah, coming home.

Where and how will you live in the second half of your life?

Most people do make major changes at various points during this phase. These changes may be driven by any number of evolving life shifts, both external and internal. Since our homes have defined us in the past, it's not surprising that, as we change, we may feel compelled to change our homes. Major changes to our surroundings such as downsizing, moving and relocating to other locales all require careful thought and planning. Making wrong choices can be extremely expensive, disappointing, and remedies may be unaffordable.

Here are a few scenarios that start the shift in thinking about home base. The realities of an "empty nest" once children are fully launched raise the questions, "Why are we heating all these rooms? And why are we living in this suburb when we could be in a condo downtown and walk to work or the theater?"

Other sentiments may bubble up out of the blue. "I can't face another New England winter — it's time to move to a gentler climate."

Or, "Gosh, the kids and grandkids are all on the West Coast and we're in Chicago. What's wrong with this picture?" And finally, "This diagnosis is serious ... and manageable, *if* I move close to family and a reputable medical center where I'll receive the care and support I'll need." Whoops! The top has just blown off Pandora's box.

As you can see, some decisions to move or relocate simply evolve while others are driven by a crisis. And, of course, decisions about our living situation are intertwined with other aspects of our lives such as our families, supportive friends, health and finances.

What is Home to You?

Let's go back to home base to start this journey.

"A home fulfills many needs: a place of self-expression, a vessel of memories, a refuge from the outside world, a cocoon where we can feel nurtured and let down our guard."
— Clare Cooper Marcus

Place ... Dwelling ... Sanctuary ... Home ... Hmm.

*What exactly is it that gives you **your** sense of being "home"?* Is it the location? The physical structure? The furnishings and collected treasures? The people there with you? Your history in that setting? The community that surrounds you? Or, all of the above and more?

The answer will be different for each of us. It's important to know your own answer to the question as it will serve to guide you in planning changes such as moving to a smaller home in town or relocating somewhere else.

Take a look at the *Home to Me Is...* exercise in Appendix G and complete it for yourself—it will help you to clarify your personal definition and meaning of home.

When you have completed this exercise and shared it with your partner or close friends, you have begun to clarify what home means to you and how you may want to approach adapting your current home or creating your next home. You can explore an incredible number of options as you search for the solution that best fits your needs, values, lifestyle and purse.

Where Do You Belong?

Finding the right community might happen naturally or it may take some introspection and effort on your part. You may decide to reside in a geographic area because of its physical attributes, and then face the task of finding kindred spirits to form your social and/or spiritual community. Many in the second half of life discover that living near children and/or grandchildren becomes the paramount driver with all other considerations being secondary. Likewise, you may determine that you need to stay close to aging parents. Or you may focus first on your spiritual community and then determine whether or not a physical move is warranted. It's complicated, and it's a very individual process, unique to each of us.

When Carol and Bill set a date to retire two years in the future, they began to research locales that might appeal. Both had lived on both coasts and in the Midwest and both had traveled extensively throughout the U.S. They had two adult children in northern California and a third in Lexington, Kentucky. Carol's mother, age 87, was living in a nursing home near their home.

Long story short, they sold their Connecticut home and moved to a small town in western Kentucky, five hours west of their daughter and her family. The attractions were the extended spring and fall seasons, the recreational opportunities (the Land between the Lakes with boating and hiking), the tax advantage (Kentucky does not tax retirement income), the dramatically lower cost of living and housing, and the availability of comparable nursing home care for Carol's mom (who relocated with them).

With proceeds from their home, Carol and Bill were able to buy a newer, bigger home with a sizable chunk left over to invest, so financially they were in good shape. They had many shared interests and both enjoyed extended periods of travel each year, including visits with family. Their biggest challenge was finding like-minded people—it took six years to build friendships with four couples, all of them "transplants" from other parts of the country. This has made their time at home more enjoyable—they are thriving in their new home.

When we consider moving to a new community we face many choices. Making good decisions can be enhanced through careful planning. Check out and complete the *Clarifying Housing and Community Preferences Checklist* in Appendix C to begin thinking in an organized way about the kind of home and community you eventually would like to find.

How's Your Social Network?

An important aspect of finding the right community involves understanding your needs and values as they relate to forming relationships with others. One of the best predictors of thriving as we age is maintaining connections and being engaged with others.

Are you single or coupled? Are you close to your family and friends? Do you see one another often? Do you bond easily with new colleagues or neighbors? If so, you may find moving to a new community an exciting and attractive option.

If it's important to you that those around you share your pastimes, your political persuasion, and your cultural interests, you will probably need to focus more on where to find those people and less on the geographic locale. Maybe you have already found them and the best choice for you will be aging in place—that is, staying in your home or your community. Again, this is a very individual choice. However, if you decide to relocate, don't forget that those who will be moving *with you* need to concur! (For more on relationships and community, see our chapter "The Relationship Dividend.")

Are You Considering Living with Family?

Are you considering a joint household with your adult children (and possibly grandchildren) or your own elderly parents? Some people find that to be a rich opportunity for intergenerational learning and sharing. It was the *only* option available in our agrarian past. If you remember TV shows like *The Waltons* or *The Real McCoys*, you witnessed that model in action. You probably recall these families had their misunderstandings and skirmishes, but everything was always happily resolved by the end of each episode. In real life, that's generally not the case.

Intergenerational living arrangements dramatically limit everyone's privacy and place tremendous demands on all family members, especially those in the middle generation. While we don't want to discourage you from embarking on this journey, we strongly recommend that you communicate deliberately and frequently about the expectations of everyone involved. Hold regular family meetings and openly air your differences and grievances.

What about Aging in Place?

According to several recent studies, most people age 50 or older feel attached to their communities, so it's not surprising that they want to remain in their own homes as they grow older. Interestingly, when people want to stay where they are, they usually do so without making a plan.

Mike and Betty are in the minority. They decided in their late 50s that they would stay in their home post retirement because their children were nearby and they were both involved in their church community. Their home was modest and on a small plot requiring relatively low maintenance and they were on schedule to pay off the mortgage in four years.

Before making the decision to stay, however, they inventoried their home, analyzing its structural soundness and the mechanicals as well as potential safety and mobility concerns should one or both of them become ill or disabled in the future. They decided to remodel, converting a formal dining room and bathroom into a master bedroom suite on the first floor, in anticipation of future needs.

Before undertaking that project and other projects, Mike and Betty de-cluttered their home from top to bottom, giving away, recycling and selling excess furniture and thirty years of accumulated "stuff." Over a period of seven years, they also replaced windows to reduce heat loss, upgraded their heating system and installed central air conditioning. They also updated the kitchen. Mike, an engineer, incorporated Universal Design (see information on UD in the resources section) features into both the kitchen and new master bath. By the time they retired, they had their dream home and plenty of free time to pursue new interests.

Universal Design is an approach to design that produces buildings, products and environments that can be used by everyone, regardless of their ability or disability. It's intended to simplify everyday life by using products and designs that create comfortable, functional and safe environments for everyone. Best of all, it allows people to remain in their homes for as long as they like. You can begin preparing your own home for the future by incorporating Universal Design elements when remodeling your kitchen or bathrooms. For example, a kitchen renovation may include kitchen counters of varying heights and placing the microwave oven at countertop height.

Other kitchen modifications can assist those with physical disabilities. Lever faucets are easier to turn off and on. Large roll-out drawers and shelves make it easier for everyone to access items stored in cabinets. Knee space built in under the sink allows a family member to sit on a stool while washing dishes. Wide doorways facilitate the navigation of a wheelchair or walker as well as make it easier to move in that new appliance. These changes allow a 10-year-old or an 80-year-old, whether standing or seated in a wheelchair, to comfortably move about the kitchen.

Bathroom remodels utilizing Universal Design concepts include a curbless shower with adjustable hand-held controls. Peter, a midlife avid runner who suddenly found himself on crutches after a recent Achilles tendon tear, was happy his remodeled bath included both features.

Non-slip surfaces on floors and bathtubs help everyone stay on their feet. Handrails and grab bars in bathrooms are also great for young and old. Lever door handles and rocker light switches support those with arthritic hands but also ease entry while carrying a laundry basket. Electrical outlets can be installed higher than usual above the floor to make them easier for everyone to reach. Exterior improvements can include brighter night-time lighting, sloped curbs on driveways for strollers and wheelchairs, and sidewalk ramps in place of stairs.

In the next 10 years, 20 percent of the U.S. population will be over the age of 65 and the number of those over 85 will triple. Making home modifications in our 50s and 60s will allow us to live safely and independently for many years to come. At the same time, the demand for new homes with Universal Design features built in is likely to skyrocket.

If a kitchen or bath remodel is in your future, you may want to consider using a Certified Aging-in-Place Specialist (CAPS) who is trained in the unique needs of the older adult population. To find a CAPS professional in your area go to the National Association of Home Builders CAPS page.

What if Life Events Impact Your Options?

If you choose to age in place, you may want to consider whether remaining at home until the end is a viable option. Retiring at age 58, Emil and Barbara moved from the home where they raised their three daughters to a one story, three bedroom cottage in a new community. Prior to moving, they spent a great deal of time researching their decision and stayed in the new community a number of weekends to make sure it was the right option for them. Their choice served them well for 20-plus years.

Eight years ago, Emil was diagnosed with Parkinson's disease. In the last few years, as he became increasingly less mobile, Emil needed Barbara's support for most of his daily activities. Unfortunately, the couple lived three hours from their nearest adult child.

At this point, the daughters became involved in their planning process. They did some research and suggested four options to their parents: 1) make modifications to the home and hire a paid caregiver, 2) move to an age 55-plus community near a daughter, 3) move to an assisted living facility or 4) move in with one of the daughters. The couple weighed the pros and cons as well as the long-term costs of each option.

Eighteen months ago, Emil and Barbara moved to an age 55+ community, five minutes from one of their daughters. The decision has been a great one—Barbara has her daughter's help caring for Emil, their new home is easier to navigate for Emil's wheelchair and walker and the couple enjoys socializing and sharing meals with their daughter, son-in-law and grandchildren.

Will this be Emil and Barbara's last home? Most likely not. The death of Emil or Barbara might necessitate another move—perhaps to a daughter's home, a nursing home or an assisted living facility. With family support and careful planning at each step, Emil and Barbara will hopefully continue, as their needs evolve, to make the best choices for them.

Emil's story reminds us that a living situation suitable for us at 60 may not work when we're 75. Changes in our physical and mental health may directly impact our housing options as we age. Divorce or the loss of a spouse are other life events that may prompt us to look for a home that better suits our changing needs. And changes in our financial status may influence decisions on the type of lifestyle and home we can truly sustain.

One planning exercise we recommend is to sit with your partner, or a close friend or family member, and consider what you might do in each of several life scenarios. We've created a *Housing Transition Choices* template in Appendix H for you to use.

If you plan to age in place, you need to consider how life transitions might affect your choices. Waiting to think about this until one of these life events occurs limits your options and may rob you of the sense of family, security, comfort and independence that make your house a home.

Models of Senior Living

When you are considering housing options, we recommend SeniorResource.com — it provides excellent descriptions of housing alternatives.

Services that Ease Transition

As we age, wherever we decide to live, we become aware of new challenges and frustrations. Solutions abound, many of which are already available, provided by an array of services that can make our lives easier and our concerned family members feel at ease. Here are a few we think worth noting:

The Village Concept: Villages are member-financed and driven, grass-roots organizations, run by volunteers and paid staff who coordinate access to affordable services — including transportation, wellness programs, home and computer repairs, social and educational activities and travel. They offer vetted and discounted providers that supplement volunteer services available in a given community. Based on the needs of their community, villages can provide anything that members want, need and can afford. Villages are spreading rapidly across the country. They complement other community approaches to aging such as Naturally Occurring Retirement Communities (NORCs) and Area Agencies on Aging Programs. Find out more about the Village Concept from resources below.

In-Home Technology for Health Monitoring: Almost 20 percent of people who care for an ill family member are willing to pay out-of-pocket for a home health monitoring service. Being able to accurately track their loved one's vital signs or detect warning signs of health decline, makes home monitoring a good solution. A survey found that over 70 percent of people caring or planning to care for a fragile senior said their primary concern was that the person in their care might take an accidental fall. In-home devices are now available that can detect a fall and call a pre-determined contact, for example, a loved one or the police. See the resource section for videos that showcase in-home technologies.

Senior Transportation Service/Ride-share/Walk-ability: Transportation is crucial to ensure that we're able to maintain an engaged lifestyle and access essential services such as medical care. Many older people who don't drive rely on family and friends to provide transportation. But for others, it's necessary to find community resources for transportation.

Transportation services vary in communities depending upon where you live. Types of transportation that may be available for elders include individual door-to-door service, fixed routes with scheduled services, and ridesharing with volunteer drivers. The Eldercare Locator (1-800-677-1116) is a good place to start your search for transportation services.

Senior Move Managers: For many of us, our adult children live a long distance from us and they and their spouses are working, making it hard for them to be involved when we're ready to move to a new living situation. Senior move managers perform a host of duties such as organizing estate and tag sales, and distributing goods to our family members and charities, sorting and packing our personal possessions, planning the interior layout in our new home, and even unpacking boxes and hanging pictures on the walls. They work with us and our families to do all, or some, of the work required for the move. A senior move manager's goal is to facilitate the physical and emotional aspects of relocation for older adults. Find a senior move manager in your area through the National Association of Senior Move Managers.

Many Choices, Many Resources

As you've seen, finding the right place for you in terms of housing, community and lifestyle is a huge theme and we have just begun the conversation. We hope that you will complete the exercises we've provided and have several open conversations with your partner, if you have one, and family and friends you trust. If you find yourself stuck or overwhelmed with the issues and options presented here, there is a lot of help available. Many life planning consultants, life coaches and registered real estate professionals specialize in working with seniors. If your local public library or Senior Center is not offering programs targeted to people 50-plus, let them know it's needed in your community and that funding may be available through the Institute of Museum and Library Services; libraries apply through their state library agency.

Be patient. As we've said, these are complex issues with many options. Your task is to decide what's best for you now and later on.

Life Planning Network Chapter Contributors

Kit Harrington Hayes, MEd, Life Planning Consultant, Founder and Principal of LifeWork Design, Author of *Managing Career Transitions,* www.KitHayes.com. (Chapter Co-Leader)

Andrea Gallagher, Certified Senior Advisor, President Senior Concerns, 2011-2012 President of Life Planning Network (LPN). www.seniorconcerns.org. (Chapter Co-Leader)

Sara Zeff Geber, PhD, Certified Retirement Options Coach, President of LifeEncore®, Author of *Fifty Plus, Minus Kids,* www. LifeEncore.com.

Dorian Mintzer, MSW, PhD, BCC, Life Transition/Retirement Coach, Licensed Third Age Coach, Co-author of *The Couples Retirement Puzzle,* www.revolutionizeretirement.com, www.couplesretirementpuzzle.com.

Roberta K. Taylor, RNCS, MEd, Certified Senior Advisor, Life Planning/Retirement Coach, Co-author of *The Couple's Retirement Puzzle,* www.pathmaking.com, www.couplesretirementpuzzle.com.

Resources

General

Clare Cooper Marcus, *House as a Mirror of Self: Exploring the Deeper Meaning of Home*, Conari Press, 1995.

Report: Housing for the 55+ Market, Trends and Insights on Boomers and Beyond, MetLife Mature Market in association with NAHB, 2009.

Richard J. Leider and David A. Shapiro, *Repacking Your Bags: Lighten Your Load for the Rest of Your Life*, Berrett-Koehler, 1995.

National Association of Senior Move Managers, www.nasmm.org.

Livable Communities

Beyond 50.05; A Report to the Nation on Livable Communities: Creating Environments for Successful Aging, AARP, 2004.

Checklist of Essential Features of Age Friendly Cities, World Health Organization, 2007.

Aging in Place

Valerie Van Booven-Whitsell, *The Senior Solution: A Family Guide to Keeping Seniors Home for Life!*, LTC Expert Publications, 2007.

AARP Housing and Mobility Publications, www.aarp.org/home-garden/livable-communities/info-05-2010/ho_order_form.html.

The MetLife Report on Aging in Place 2.0: Rethinking Solutions to the Home Care Challenge, MetLife Mature Market Institute in association with Louis Tenenbaum, CAPS, CAASH, 2010, www.metlife.com/mmi/research/aging-in-place.html?SCOPE=Metlife#insights.

Housing for a Lifetime, MIT AgeLab, 2011, www.youtube.com/wat ch?v=v1UyQ9wIBos&feature=related.

National Association of Home Builders, www.nahb.org.

The National Resource Center on Supportive Housing and Home Modifications provides information and resources for professionals and consumers, www.homemods.org.

Videos that showcase in-home technologies, www.leadingage.org/ Imagine-the-Future-of-Aging.aspx.

Alternative Housing

The Consumer Guide to Senior Housing, Society of Certified Senior Advisors, 2011.

Senior Resource, www.seniorresource.com/house.htm.

Village Concept, www.vtvnetwork.org.

Living in 3D — Enrich Your Life With Purpose, Legacy and Spirituality

Have you thought about the following BIG questions?

- What is my purpose in life?

- How will I leave the world a little better for coming generations? What will be my legacy?

- How can I honor and expand my spiritual connection?

A Timeless Pursuit

Having a sense of purpose, a commitment to something outside of ourselves, is central to living a fulfilling, engaged life. That's especially true as we age. Our increasing life expectancy — now 33 years greater than a century ago — offers us a novel opportunity to discover and embrace our purpose in the second half of life, to leave a meaningful legacy and to connect with something greater than ourselves.

Adult development psychologists tell us there is something about passing midlife that "pushes" us beyond such fundamental tasks as parenting and productivity to seek meaning and authenticity. Our motivating force shifts from success to significance.

However we define purpose, the search for it often leads to these questions: What do I want to contribute to make the world a little better? What legacies will I leave for succeeding generations?

For many, this post-midlife concern for purpose and legacy may point to a path of greater spirituality. We may initiate a connection with a spiritual power or wisdom, however we understand it: God, Spirit, All That Is, Nature or the Great Mystery. Possessing a larger purpose helps us to see a bigger, less ego-driven picture of the world and our unique role in it. It gives us a clearer vision for how, using our most authentic self, we can live with integrity and serve.

As Ron Pevny, certified Sage-ing leader, writes in "The Inner Work of Eldering," exploring purpose and meaning helps us do the inner work of reclaiming our best, whole self. It helps us to release old baggage that saps energy and joy and sabotages our best intentions. It guides us to act and live with more intentionality. Almost automatically, we model positive aging and leave positive legacies for those we know and touch now — and for those later we will never know.

Purpose — What Is It?

Ask yourself:

- Why am I here? What's my life about?

- What do I really want to do with my time, money and talents?

Imagine purpose as an internal compass that helps you to find your way no matter where you are or what the circumstances of your life.

Purpose — defined as our reason for being, calling, mission or vocation — encompasses our deepest values, talents and passions. It underlies our contribution to life and is expressed through our interactions with family, community, friendships, in our work, and through creative and spiritual activities.

How do I find my purpose at this point in my life?

While some seem to grasp their purpose effortlessly, for others, discovering their purpose can seem elusive. Some believe that we choose our purpose. Others believe purpose is born into us and it is our job to discover it. Whatever your belief, the search for purpose can itself become a highly purposeful and productive activity. Often, it isn't until we invest ourselves in this quest that we uncover the missing piece to our personal puzzle.

For example, as financial marketer Dana Dakin, of Wilmot Flat, New Hampshire, approached her 60th birthday, she spent an entire year asking everyone she met what meaningful project she might undertake. A chance encounter at an art fair led Dakin to study microfinance, travel to Africa and commit herself to founding a micro-lending program in Pokuase, Ghana. She sold her used Volvo for $5000 of seed money, gathered the support of neighbors in New Hampshire, and kept going back. In less than a decade, WomensTrust became a model for cooperative aid programs in Africa, writes Bruce Frankel in *What Should I Do With the Rest of My Life? True Stories of Finding Success, Passion and New Meaning in the Second Half of Life.*

We believe that clues to your purpose can be found in your experiences. Chances are you already experience times when you feel as if you are living *on purpose.* You feel at your best, engaged and energized, in flow and focused, and having an impact that fulfills you. Reviewing such times is a great place to begin exploring your purpose.

Uncovering your life purpose is not a "one shot deal," Richard Leider writes in *The Power of Purpose.* Rather, it's a process of self-discovery and self-acceptance that poses clarifying questions, such as:

- What concerns or life conditions provoke strong emotions, capture my attention or spur me to act?

- Which of my gifts or strengths do I want to use regardless of the activity?

The main ingredient in the process of finding your purpose is spending time with the person who has the answers: You! Once you've decided to explore your purpose you may choose one of several routes. You can explore by yourself with the help of many available online tools (see our chapter on "Your Life Lessons"), self-help books or guided audio programs, such as *The Purpose of Your Life Experiential Guide* by Carol Adrienne or The Roadmap to Meaningful Midlife® audio/workbook program by Mary Radu, certified professional coach, and Cheryl Mann. If you choose this route, we suggest you find a trusted "buddy" with whom you can share your progress. Alternatively, consider getting guidance from a coach or other life planning professional.

How will finding purpose affect my life, my relationships, my ability to meet my financial obligations and personal needs?

When individuals are living purposefully, they often describe being in *flow*, experiencing synchronicity, having events and outcomes fall into place. They describe feeling more energy, enthusiasm and satisfaction. And because they're in sync with what they're doing, they are more successful at it. Feeling fulfilled, even in only one area of your life, fuels positive changes in your relationships, work, health and leisure activities.

Making life changes often feels risky. But guided by purpose, decision-making becomes less stressful. Only you can decide what choices are right for you. If you can't change your financial circumstances, for example, or you're unwilling to make changes that your significant other may not like, then make choices that honor those parameters and work within them. If, on the other hand, you are prepared and eager to shift your life dramatically, you may make more radical choices.

For instance, when retired intelligence officer Thomas Dwyer, of Taneytown, Maryland, told his family that he was going to become a modern dancer, his daughter said it was as if someone had walked into the living room and announced, "I think I will take a Sunday drive to the moon." But Dwyer, whose story is also chronicled in Frankel's *What Should I Do With the Rest of My Life?*, succeeded and continues more than twenty years later to work as a principal dancer for a major intergenerational dance company.

Remember, it's not always necessary to change a job to live your purpose. You can develop aspects of your current position or activities outside of work to express your purpose. Or simply be more intentional in your interactions with others in daily life.

Purpose is not a job, role or goal. It is holding and living the belief that each of our lives, our part in the whole of things, matters.

Ask yourself:

- How will living more purposefully change my life?

- What changes am I willing to make? What am I unwilling to change?

Once you've discovered your purpose, consider some tried and true methods others have found helpful for staying on the path.

- Write a purpose statement or create a picture that symbolizes your purpose. Post this where you will see it on waking and throughout the day.

- Practice self-care to help stay focused, healthy and fulfilled.

- Integrate purpose into your life by honoring all parts of yourself, including the foundational aspects — economic sufficiency, health, emotional well-being.

- Devise strategies to deal with activities that distract you from your purpose.

- Incorporate new activities to bring you into closer alignment with your purpose.

- Break down big goals and tasks into baby steps that you can do in a reasonable amount of time, such as a week.

- Notice how the quality of your experience changes. Savor the goodness!

- Seek support from other like-minded individuals with whom you can share your purpose and passion.

Legacy—How Do I Create Mine?

As our time horizon draws closer in the second half of life, a new set of questions may increasingly preoccupy us. What am I doing to leave the world a little better than I found it? What wisdom and life lessons am I passing on to the next generation? How do I want to be remembered? How do I want to serve the future?

The dictionary definition of "legacy" (a gift or bequest of property) is narrow and concrete. We propose a broader definition. Legacy is anything, tangible or intangible, that we gift, bequeath or leave behind, intentionally or unintentionally, during our life or at our death. It's the lasting imprint of our life that ripples into succeeding generations.

If you consider all the legacies (some undoubtedly more positive than others) you have received, you'll realize no one can help but leave legacies. We leave them as the memory of our essence, in actions that live on in others' memories and actions, and in various records we leave behind.

What's the point in planning our legacies if we inevitably leave them behind anyway?

The key to living and leaving positive legacies is the concept of "legacies of the heart," a phrase coined by Donna Krone, True Purpose™ coach, and Meg Newhouse, certified life coach, to describe legacies stemming from our essential, highest, wisest self. Such legacies reflect compassion, acceptance, generosity and forgiveness. "Legacies of the heart" are true gifts—a gift of yourself without strings or expectations. In simplest terms, they are legacies born from love.

By living as much as possible from our heart, soul or center, we also prevent leaving harmful, hurtful legacies—those fed by fear-based instincts such as competition, lack, exclusion and domination. Although we have little control over the legacies that have come our way, we have a great deal of choice about what we do with them.

How can I figure out what legacies to leave?

Ask yourself:

- What does the world need that calls forth my natural talents?

- What values, wisdom and life lessons do I want to pass on?

- What specific, tangible things do I want to leave behind?

For Thomas Dwyer, the impulse to become a dancer arrived as a vision of his legacy when, one day, he attended an elder dance performance for high school students. The students' amazement triggered Dwyer's epiphany. He became determined to show younger generations that they didn't have to live out old age in a rocking chair. Dana Dakin and her WomensTrust legacy is evolving. It will result from having empowered the women of Pokuase to become financially self-sufficient and from supporting educational opportunities for the village's girls, its next generation of women.

By being clearer about who you really are and who you are becoming, and by letting your unique values, gifts, dreams, passion and purpose guide your daily choices, you will live your best legacy — *now.* This is not something to postpone to your deathbed!

If you still need help with clarifying your legacy, adult mentor Dick Haid suggests creating your own personal advisory board of diverse people who know and will champion you. They'll ask you powerful questions and help you generate options.

Keep in mind that people whose lives you have touched directly often want tangible reminders to help them remember and to pass on. Without tangible expression, much of our "internal wealth" may remain buried, depriving future generations of the chance to connect to their personal and cultural roots.

You may already have a desire to leave behind material "legacies of the heart," including written, aural or visual evidence of your passions, purpose and life lessons. If you haven't, perhaps now is the time to begin "saving" your life — in the computer, not the theological sense — for coming generations, as Age-ing to Sage-ing author Rabbi Zalman Schachter-Shalomi suggests.

Which tangible, personal "legacies of the heart" call to you?

1. Photo scrapbooks or digitally published books with text commemorating important family or other events

2. Memoirs

3. Videos of special events

4. Family histories, genealogy

5. Heirlooms or prized possessions with notes about their history and meaning

6. Family recipes, and food and holiday traditions

7. Artistic creations, such as quilts, paintings, collages, woodworking

8. Ethical wills, legacy letters or other structured writings bequeathing "internal wealth" (also see the discussion on legacy in our final chapter)

9. Financial or material gifts to prized individuals, organizations and causes.

When will you start?

Although we advocate being intentional and starting sooner rather than later, it's never too late to begin! We leave our legacies through our last breath. Seeing through the lens of legacy strengthens our sense of purpose and meaning and thereby energizes us. What of your current harvest does your heart want to pass on? What do you need to express, do or give for you to feel complete?

"And the only measure of your words and your deeds
Will be the love you leave behind when you're done."
— Fred Small's "Everything Possible"

Spiritual Promptings—How Do I Answer Them?

"To be human is to be lost in the woods," writes Elizabeth Lesser, in *Broken Open: How Difficult Times Can Help Us Grow*. "None of us arrives here with clear directions on how to get from point A to point B without stumbling into the forest of confusion or catastrophe or wrongdoing. Although they are dark and dangerous, it is in the woods that we discover our strengths."

Ask yourself:

* Who am I and why am I here?

* What will bring meaning into my life?"

* Is there something wiser or bigger than myself that I can count on for guidance and support?

These questions often arise in times of shifting circumstances, major crises or life transitions. They might be provoked by the curiosity or challenge of a loved one, teacher, friend or child. They might be heard in the "still small voice" that persists when we slow down our busy lives. They might be "felt" — pondered in the heart without language — and create yearning. Some say their deepest questions are surrounded by a kind of "luminescence" or energy. Most say these questions are persistent, even nagging. Aging is their universal catalyst. Facing loss, becoming aware of our mortality, embracing new love, retiring from our work lives, losing energy or capacity, losing loved ones to death — all can make us acutely aware of questions lying just below the surface.

Ask yourself:

- What is one of the deepest, most persistent questions for *me* right now?

- What words or images do I associate with this question? Record them.

Spiritual Quest

These spiritual questions can be compelling, but also tend to be uncomfortable. They require us to shift gears, to question our thoughts and behaviors. It's easy to fall into a mindless pattern of pushing them aside and focusing on more "pressing concerns." By contrast, spirituality is the intentional turning toward these questions. We allow the answers to resonate in our hearts and minds, shape our values, and guide our daily choices. Deepening our spirituality enables us to believe and trust as we walk through unfamiliar territory in our lives.

How do I develop spirituality if I'm not a religious person?

Engaging in a religious tradition can be a rewarding path for spiritual growth and development, but it's not for everyone. Answering the deepest questions doesn't require a specific philosophy or belief system. It does require courage, grit, curiosity and self-reflection. Don't let the word "spiritual" get in your way. If it doesn't work for you, find another word or phrase that does. It is the practices, the things you choose to do, that become the doorways to discovering the answers to those nagging questions.

Roger Walsh, a professor of psychiatry, philosophy and anthropology, describes seven central practices for developing spirituality in his book, *Essential Spirituality*. Framed in non-religious language, these are practices that all world religions have in common:

- Transform your motivation—learn to reduce cravings and attachments that do not really satisfy deeper needs, while discovering deeper desires (purpose).

- Cultivate emotional wisdom—heal your heart and learn to love.

- Live ethically—feel good by doing good.

- Increase concentration—calm your mind.

- Awaken spiritual vision—see clearly and recognize the sacred in all things.

- Enrich spiritual intelligence—develop wisdom and understand life.

- Express spirit in action—embrace generosity and the joy of service.

How can I create a meaningful daily practice?

Do you yearn to engage in a spiritual practice of some sort, a regular activity that will help you grow into your deepest purpose? Do you also believe that you don't have the time, the discipline, or the worthiness to begin? You are not alone!

You may not realize that you have already begun a practice. The yearning itself is an awakening. Acknowledging it to yourself and to others is another important step. A daily practice can honor this yearning by providing a steady and nourishing anchor that allows your awakening to grow and deepen over time. When beginning a spiritual practice, take small steps so you can savor the process.

What do we mean by a "practice"?

"A spiritual or growth-fostering practice includes three elements: intention, regular repetition and presence," writes Natalie Eldridge, psychologist and life transition coach, in her *Action on Purpose* newsletter. It is the intentional development of a habit through regular repetition and readiness to approach each repetition with freshness and an open heart.

We have already developed many intentional habits or rituals, such as brushing our teeth, making lunch or driving a car. As we learn these activities, we give them our active attention. Once familiar, we are less likely to do so. The fresh attention of mindfulness makes an intentional practice into a spiritual practice.

Some common forms of spiritual practice include prayer, meditation, reflective journaling, dietary practices, chanting, yoga, tai chi, dance, social action, artistic endeavors and communing with nature. Communities of worship (religious services) or spiritual support groups, meditation groups and yoga classes provide opportunities to practice with others regularly. The paths toward spiritual development are many and diverse.

In developing your daily practice, pay attention to what you feel drawn to do. You may want to revisit a practice learned in childhood, bringing fresh meaning and intention to it. You may be drawn to try new practices. Those that help you honor the questions in your heart will be most meaningful for you.

Ask yourself:

- What is one practice I will do each day to honor my spiritual questions?

Becoming Whole

All the dimensions of our lives are supported by the commitment to personal and spiritual growth explored in this chapter. Having financial security, physical health or a good housing situation only brings real joy if accompanied by a sense of purpose and wholeness. Living on purpose brings joy that can compensate for ill health or less than ideal living conditions. Indeed, research shows that adults who have a sense of purpose enjoy better health, more social engagement and greater happiness in their later years.

As we make the second-half-of-life shift from externally defined success to internally defined significance, the connections between purpose, legacy and spirituality become undeniably clear. If we live authentically and on purpose, we will inevitably leave legacies of the heart and become attentive to and guided by the larger mystery of life.

We invite you to spend some time reflecting on your priorities in the areas of purpose, legacy and spirituality. Remember, you just need to commit to taking one step at a time. We believe the results will be worth your time and effort. And you'll be closer to answering "yes" to the three cardinal questions from Elisabeth Kübler-Ross, the Swiss American psychiatrist and pioneer in end-of-life concerns:

- Have I given and received love?
- Have I lived my life (as opposed to someone else's)?
- Have I left the world a little better than I found it?

Life Planning Network Chapter Contributors

Margaret (Meg) Newhouse, PhD, CPCC, Certified Life Coach, Founder of the Life Planning Network, Author of *Life Planning for the Third Age*, www.passionandpurpose.com. (Chapter Leader)

Natalie Eldridge, PhD, Psychologist and Life Transition Coach, Author of *Action on Purpose* Newsletter, www.EldridgeWorks.com.

Bruce Frankel, Author of *What Should I Do With the Rest of My Life? True Stories of Finding Success, Passion and New Meaning in the Second Half of Life*, www.brucefrankel.net.

Dick Haid, PhD, PCC, Adult Mentor, www.adultmentor.com.

Donna Krone, CPCC, Certified True Purpose™ Coach/Facilitator, www.sacredconversations.com.

Ron Pevny, MA, Life Coach, Certified Sage-ing Leader, Founder of the Center for Conscious Eldering, www.centerforconsciouseldering.com.

Mary Radu, MS, MSW, CPCC, Certified Professional Coach, Philanthropy Mentor and author of *The Roadmap to Meaningful Midlife*®, www.pathmakercoaching.com.

Resources

Purpose

Carol Adrienne, *The Purpose of Your Life Experiential Guide*, William Morrow, 1998.

Barry K. Baines, *Ethical Wills: Putting Your Values on Paper*, Perseus Publishing, 2001.

Bruce Frankel, *What Should I Do With the Rest of My Life? True Stories of Finding Success, Passion and New Meaning in the Second Half of Life*, Penguin, 2010.

Tim Kelley, *True Purpose: 12 Strategies for Discovering the Difference You are Meant to Make*, Transcendent Solutions Press, 2009.

Richard J. Leider, *The Power of Purpose: Find Meaning, Live Longer, Better*, Berrett-Koehler, Publishers, 2010. Tools for discovering core gifts/purpose can be found at www. inventuregroup.com.

Dawna Markova, *I Will Not Die an Unlived Life: Reclaiming Purpose and Passion*, Conari Press, 2000.

Parker J. Palmer, *Let Your Life Speak: Listening for the Voice of Vocation*, Harper-Collins, 2000.

Mary Radu and Cheryl Mann, *The Roadmap to Meaningful Midlife®: Create Your Vision and Action Plan (Audio/pdf Workbook)*, 2007.

Eckhart Tolle, *A New Earth: Awakening Your Life's Purpose*, Penguin, 2008.

Richard Haid, Thomas Mraz, Caitlin Williams, *Third Quarter of Life Guide* and Card Sorts, www.adultmentor.com/3qlcs.html.

Legacy

Gloria Burgess, *Dare to Wear Your Soul on the Outside: Live Your Legacy Now*, Jossey-Bass, 2008.

Rachel Freed, *Women's Lives, Women's Legacies: Passing Your Beliefs and Blessings to Future Generations*, Fairview Press, 2003.

Dennis Ledoux, *The Photo Scribe, A Writing Guide: How to Write the Stories Behind Your Photographs*, Soleil Press, 2008. *Turning Memories into Memoirs: A Handbook for Writing Life Stories*, Soleil Press, 2005.

Margaret (Meg) Newhouse, Legacies of the Heart, *Itineraries ezine*, Summer, 2009, www.secondjourney.org.

Alan Seale, *Soul Mission, Life Vision: Recognize Your True Gifts and Make Your Mark in the World,* Red Wheel/Weiser, 2003.

The Legacy Center, online guide to identify and communicate core values and experiences that give life meaning, www.thelegacycenter.net.

Story Corps provides Americans of all backgrounds and beliefs with the opportunity to record, share and preserve the stories of their lives, www.storycorps.org.

Spirituality

Ram Dass, *Still Here: Embracing Aging, Changing, and Dying,* Riverhead Press, 2000.

Dwight H. Judy, *Discerning Life Transitions: Listening Together in Spiritual Direction,* Morehouse Publishing, 2010.

Elizabeth Lesser, *Broken Open: How Difficult Times Can Help Us Grow,* Villard Books, 2004.

Ron Pevny, The Inner Work of Eldering, *Itineraries ezine,* Spring, 2011, www.secondjourney.org.

Zalman Schachter-Shalomi and Ronald S. Miller, *From Age-ing to Sage-ing: A Profound New Vision of Growing Older,* Warner Books, 1997, www.sage-ingguild.org.

Roger Walsh, *Essential Spirituality: The 7 Central Practices to Awaken Heart and Mind,* Wiley and Sons, 1999.

Harry (Rick) Moody, *Human Values in Aging* monthly newsletter, International Longevity Center — USA.

Itineraries ezine, published quarterly by Second Journey, www.secondjourney.org.

Conscious Aging Alliance, ten organizations that focus on spirituality and legacy in later life.

Awaken Your Creativity — Finding your fun, passion and the artist within

REMEMBER THE "GOLDEN YEARS"? Our parents may have dreamed about retiring at age 65 to a 24/7 leisure lifestyle with a reliable pension in the Sun Belt. That's not possible or even desirable for most of us.

In this period of great change, coming both from inside as well as the environment in which we live, we want to have the choice to slow down, to travel, to learn to play a musical instrument or a new sport, or to spend more time with family. For many of us, we also want to continue to earn income. Now we have the opportunity to revisit the balance of learning, leisure, play, creativity *and* work, with the benefit of new skills, greater self-knowledge and the perspective born of having lived many decades. This period in our lives may be the *most* creative, especially if we have not had the opportunity to express ourselves in our work.

This chapter is not only about exercising choice, but about how and why we *need* to refashion our expectations of retirement that are based on our parents' experience. If we don't, we may risk physical decline, depression and cognitive deficiencies. The good news is that by keeping our brains fit, we invite a whole lot more fun, creativity and meaning into our lives.

Ask yourself these questions:

* How can I keep stretching my mind to protect, and even build, brainpower?

* How do I want to define my leisure time to express my values and passions, rather than living a humdrum life?

* How can accessing my creativity increase my physical, emotional and social well-being?

* How can I imbue more areas of my life with a playful, creative attitude and why is this important to my fulfillment as I age?

These questions are relevant to our lives whether we are 50, 75 or 95 and represent a sea change from the way the previous generation thought about leisure and aging.

The Adult Brain—Use It or Lose It

Twenty-first century research shows that brain cells can develop and regenerate throughout life. Research using MRIs demonstrates that by exercising our remarkable brain, we can increase the development of new neural connections that make us more alert, more productive and more fulfilled until old, old age. This is known as *neuroplasticity*. So, we need to redefine "senior moment" to mean our having a creative insight, advancing in our tennis game, or writing a poem for a loved one.

Even though the brain starts to lose some functioning starting as early as 45, it gains in other ways. Older people recognize the big picture better than young people. We perceive patterns and see the significance of things more easily. Our judgment and ability to "read" people improves with age. We also mellow, which means that our emotions are not as raw; we tend to see things in better perspective. This helps us to be more open to new experiences, less distracted by the tumultuous feelings of youth.

Barbara Strauch, *The New York Times* health and sciences editor and author of *The Secret Life of the Grown-Up Brain,* writes that we are programmed to grow wiser and more cheerful as we age. Something to look forward to! There's also evidence from surveys that young people see us in a different light now than they did when "don't trust anyone over 30" was in vogue. "Awesome," say the 30-somethings at the cable access TV station where TV host and life coach Karma Kitaj produces *Alivelihood: New Adventures as We Age.* "I like to brag to them that I mastered yet another techno-hurdle in formatting my show for syndication."

Exercising our brains for cognitive and emotional health

These experiences are "chocolate for the brain."

Just as we consider the triceps and quad muscles in our arms and legs, we can think of our brain as a muscle that requires exercise to maintain its strength and agility. We stimulate our brains to form multiple connections either by doing something novel or by deepening experiences that we know well. So, for example, Kitaj, who started riding horses at age 50, takes lessons weekly to get more agile and fit. We don't need to start a whole new activity to increase those neural connections in our brains. How can we exercise our brains?

- Challenge your brain to *learn something new,* not to do the same old things. This creates more proliferation of connections that reduce the risk of Alzheimer's and other dementias. Learn a new language, sport, game, creative activity, or deepen familiar ones by practicing new aspects of what you already love to do.

- Combine mental with physical learning. Take up or expand your golf game, tennis, horseback riding, zumba dance, yoga.

- Read and talk with people with dissenting opinions, not just those with whom you agree. Jack Mezirow, from Columbia Teachers College in New York, says that giving yourself a "disorienting dilemma" helps you to critically reflect on the assumptions you've acquired.

- Boost brain *and* immune system by mastering challenges one small step at a time.

- Engage in lifelong learning by seeking out adult learning centers in community colleges or the Osher Lifelong Learning Institutes that exist in most major colleges across the country.

What are you willing to do today to stretch your brain, to learn something new? See Kitaj's blog, *Retirement as You Want It* for more articles about brain vitality.

Quality Active Leisure Pursuits

- Writing, including journaling

- Reading

- Exercising

- Walking in nature

- Painting, drawing, sculpting

- Creating new recipes

- Gardening

- Dancing

- Playing any sport

- Taking a course

- Traveling with purpose rather than being a tour bus tourist

- Daydreaming, meditating, or reflecting can also engage us in an active way

(From *The Joy of Not Working*)

Leisure—Boring or Energizing?

> *"Retirement is when you stop living at work*
> *and begin working at living."*
> *— Author unknown*

Most people are negligent about how they use their leisure time. Ernie J. Zelinski, leisure expert and author of *The Joy of Not Working: A Book for the Retired, Unemployed, and Overworked,* believes that all but the most creative among us are unhappy in their leisure. They mistake leisure for being a couch potato or a beach bum, i.e., doing passive activities or none at all.

Quality leisure, Zelinski writes, is dependent upon a feeling of *challenge* and a *sense of accomplishment.* People who are most fulfilled in their leisure are those who spend a good deal of their time experiencing life *actively* — instead of watching hours of TV, drinking, overeating, shopping and watching spectator sports.

To feel energized by leisure, rather than bored, we need to "master the moment," to *live mindfully,* Zelinski writes. People who do so experience qualities of "Flow," a term coined by psychologist Mihaly Csikszentmihalyi:

- They are engaged and focused

- They find the activity to be *challenging but doable* — feeling neither anxious nor bored

- They have a sense of serenity — with little self-consciousness

- They are less aware of time passing

- They find the process is more important than the outcome

Leisure is an inner state of being. It has a contemplative aspect, a quieting of the soul, a time when one is open and receptive to inner and outer stimuli, but not overwhelmed by them. We advocate creating a rhythm of activity and contemplation to experience the most satisfying leisure. "Rather than multi-tasking, which has come to be the hallmark of non-leisure, cultivate a habit of *mono-tasking* — one thing at a time," says Margaret Hothem, Leisure Studies Professor at Gordon College.

Carl Honoré, author of *In Praise of Slow,* advocates *savoring,* allowing oneself to fully experience the present moment. Neuroscientists have found, he writes, that when we are in this slower state of mind, we're able to be more creative, because the brain "slips into a deeper, richer, more nuanced mode of thought."

What will you do today to nurture that kind of state of mind for yourself? How will you create more attention to the moment, more focus, and more freedom?

One thing you can do is awaken your creative self.

Is Creativity Reserved for the Gifted?

The late esteemed gerontologist, Gene D. Cohen, MD, said in *The Creative Age: Awakening Human Potential in the Second Half of Life,* that "the potential for creativity in the second half of life is not the exception, but the rule." Creativity is not reserved for the gifted. We all have an "instinct for exploring, for enjoying novelty and risk," Csikszentmihalyi writes in *Flow*. It's our curiosity that leads to creativity. Although we were born with this propensity, Csikszentmihalyi believes it can "wither on the vine" if not used. How many of us haven't painted a picture since we were in kindergarten? We can resurrect our childlike creativity just by exposing ourselves to creative opportunities.

Little "c" Creativity

- Creating a new recipe
- Making a scrapbook for family memories
- Choosing beautiful things for the home
- Costuming ourselves
- Composing a poem for a friend's birthday
- Creating a party for a friend
- Designing a book of family memories online

We all can access our creativity, but many are *stuck in the habit of "non-creativity."* The Harvard psychologist Howard Gardner, who proposed the theory of multiple intelligences, distinguished between little "c" and big "C" creativity. Big C refers to the extraordinary accomplishments of artists, inventors, and scientists. Little "c" refers to the "diversity of everyday activities and accomplishments ... by ordinary people who may never become famous but are nonetheless extremely creative in their pursuits," explains Cohen in *The Creative Age*.

We can foster a habit of creativity by exposing ourselves to different situations where we can experiment and take risks with new learning, new mediums, new forms of movement. Judith-Kate Friedman, founder of Songwriting Works, says "brain science finds that music lights up the brain almost more than any other human activity." What lights up on brain MRIs signifies how much of the brain area we're using. The more, the better.

Kitaj grew up with a much older brother who became an internationally known painter early in his life. Because of this, she imagined that artist, genius and early signs of "talent" went hand in hand. "I saw no hint of the creative artist in myself," says Kitaj. "It wasn't until last year when I interviewed creativity coach Sandra Shuman for my TV show and went to her studio for a collage workshop, that I 'discovered' my creativity." Since then Kitaj has developed her own studio and had her debut art show after just one year of painting. *We are* **all** *budding artists!*

Why living creatively is not only fun, but good for us:

- It increases the proliferation of neural connections that keep us mentally fit until the day we die. It's associated with preventing cognitive degeneration.

- It gives us energy and engages us while offering the possibility of becoming deeply involved in activities.

- It gives us a sense of meaning and purpose, which is connected to well-being in many research studies.

- It allows us to make new connections with people who are also living creatively. Establishing and maintaining a social network is correlated with greater well-being and longevity.

- It gives focus and structure to our leisure time.

Researchers have documented what happens when we engage creatively as we age. Here are findings from two of the studies:

▪ Dr. Cohen conducted one of the first scientific studies of the impact of participation in intensive creativity programs on health and well-being. He studied people aged 65-100 who engaged in creativity programs and compared them to a group of people who were not offered the creative programs. The positive findings of the participants were significant and continued at a two-year follow-up. They included: 1) an increase in overall health after one year; 2) a decrease in doctor visits and medication usage, and 3) fewer falls.

▪ Helga and Tony Noice, who received the 2010 Dr. Gene D. Cohen Research Award in Creativity from the National Center for Creative Aging (NCCA), studied the effect of participation in theater arts in people over age 60 and compared them to a group that had no exposure to acting. They looked at the impact on their cognitive functioning and psychological well-being. They found stunning improvement in cognitive functioning and psychological well-being after only eight one-hour acting sessions. They believe it's the multi-sensory of acting that produced this result.

"Twenty years from now you will be more disappointed by the things you didn't do than by the ones you did do. So throw off the bowlines. Sail away from the safe harbor. Catch the trade winds in your sails. Explore. Dream. Discover."

– Mark Twain

The NCCA lists programs and research studies across the country. Educator and social entrepreneur, Jan Hively, spearheaded one of the innovative projects, the Minnesota Creative Arts & Aging Network (MnCAAN). Employing professional artists as teachers, MnCAAN expands opportunities for the active, creative expression of older adults. Hively says, "As illustrated in the NCCA listings, people feel better about themselves and about aging when they engage regularly in dance, painting, sculpture, theater, writing—anything that gets their creative juices flowing." See Hively's film, *The Creative Power of Aging*, which illustrates the benefits of creative expression for older adults.

How will you take action to release your creative juices? Try playing more.

Is Play Just for Children?

What is play? Boston College psychologist Peter Gray, PhD, has studied the value of play in children and adults. Play, he writes, involves a *mental attitude*, not a specific form of behavior. This is why many people can be playful at work or while taking care of their grandchildren, while others find those activities to be routine or even drudgery. Gray suggests that play is essential in adults. So, by changing our mindset, *we can learn to be playful in any aspect of our lives*—for example, exercising, cooking, going to work or golfing.

You can view Dr. Stuart Brown's TED lecture online for an amusing and comprehensive view about the critical importance of play for adults. Brown became aware of the dangers of play deprivation when he studied the childhood histories of the Texas Tower shooter and other murderers. He became convinced that we sacrifice play at our peril. As humans, Brown says, we are constitutionally capable of neoteny, the capacity to retain childlike qualities throughout life. It allows us to be flexible, imaginative, and creative in problem-solving. It explains why so many adults flock to Disneyland or love pets and sports.

With the onset of this new age, the second half of life, we're inclined to feel "It's now or never," or "Now I can wear purple." Last year, Kitaj joined an improvisational acting workshop led by Boston improv guru Daena Giardella. Although scary at first, since she'd never done any acting before, Giardella created a welcoming and safe atmosphere. "Now I've become an improv groupie," says Kitaj.

> *Give yourself permission*
> *to have a playful attitude*
> *in whatever you do.*

How can we put this cutting-edge research and scholarly writing about learning, leisure and creativity into practice in our daily lives?

Here are five suggestions to traverse the second half of our lives more joyously and playfully:

- Identify and deepen daily practices for contemplation, mindfulness and slowing down.

- Create Flow experiences.

- Give yourself permission to experiment, do novel things and take risks to expand your brain capacity.

- Commune and collaborate with other like-minded people who want to stretch their learning and repertoire of creative activities.

- If you're stuck, engage a life planning coach to help you get clarity about what your passions are, to encourage you to experiment and take reasonable risks, and to be accountable to what you want to do in this exciting new stage of life.

Life Planning Network Chapter Contributors

Karma Kitaj, PhD, Certified Life Coach, Psychotherapist, Artist, Author of *Women Who Could… and Did: Stories of 26 Exemplary Artists & Scientists,* www.LifeSpringCoaching.com, www. RetirementAsYouWantIt.com. (Chapter Leader)

Kendall Dudley, MA, Career and Life Design Consultant, www.kendalldudley.com.

Judith-Kate Friedman, Author of "The Songwriting Works ™ Model" in Hartman-Stein & LaRue, *Enhancing Cognitive Fitness in Adults*, Springer, 2011, www.Songwritingworks.org.

Jan Hively, PhD, Educator and Social Entrepreneur, www.mncaan.net.

Margaret "Peggy" Hothem, EdD, Professor of Leisure and Recreational Studies, Gordon College, www.Gordon.edu.

Fred Mandell, PhD, Creative Catalyst, Artist, Co-author of *Becoming a Life Change Artist: 7 Creative Skills to Reinvent Yourself at Any Stage of Life*, www.fredmandell.com.

Resources

General

Mihaly Csikszentmihalyi, *Flow: The Psychology of Optimal Experience*, Harper & Row Publishers, 1990, Part 1 and Chapters 3-7.

Richard J. Leider, *The Power of Purpose: Find Meaning, Live Longer, Better,* Berrett-Koehler, Publishers, 2010, Chapters 3-4.

Learning

Gene D. Cohen, *The Mature Mind: The Positive Power of the Aging Brain,* Basic Books, 2005.

Hartman-Stein and Asenath LaRue, editors, *Enhancing Cognitive Fitness In Adults: A Guide To The Use And Development Of Community-Based Programs,* Springer, 2011.

Karma Kitaj, www.RetirementAsYouWantIt.com (blog), see Interviews.

Jack Mezirow, *Learning as Transformation,* Jossey-Bass, 2000.

Osher Life Long Learning Institutes, http://usm.maine.edu/olli/national.

Barbara Strauch, *The Secret Life of the Grown-Up Brain: The Surprising Talents of the Middle-Aged Mind,* Viking Penguin, 2010.

Leisure

Carl Honorè, *In Praise of Slow: How a World Wide Movement is Challenging the Cult of Speed,* Orion Books, 2004.

Ernie J. Zelinski, *The Joy of Not Working: A Book for the Retired, Unemployed and Overworked,* Ten Speed Press, 1997, Chapters 1, 5 6.

Zelinski, Ernie J., *How to Retire Happy, Wild, and Free,* Visions International Publishing, 2009, Chapters 7 and 9.

Creativity

Gene D. Cohen, *The Creative Age: Awakening Human Potential in the Second Half of Life,* Avon Books, 2000, Chapters 4-7.

Mihaly Csikszentmihalyi, *Creativity: Flow and the Psychology of Discovery & Invention,* Harper Row, 1996, Parts 1 and 3.

Judith-Kate Friedman, www.songwritingworks.org.

Howard Gardner, *Five Minds for the Future,* Harvard Business School Press, 2006.

Jan Hively, "The Creative Power of Aging" (film), www.mncaan.net/community/community-events-cm-film.html.

Karma Kitaj, *Women Who Could... and Did: Stories of 26 Exemplary Artists & Scientists,* Huckle Hill Press, 2002.

Fred Mandell, *Becoming a Life Change Artist: 7 Creative Skills to Reinvent Yourself at Any Stage of Life,* The Penguin Group, 2010,

Chapter 2 and all of Parts 2 and 3.

National Center for Creative Aging (NCCA), www.creativeaging.org.

Helga and Tony Noice, recipients of 2010 Dr. Gene D. Cohen Research Award in Creativity from the NCCA, www. creativeaging.org.

Play

Stuart Brown, *Play: How it Shapes the Brain, Opens the Imagination and Invigorates the Soul,* The Penguin Group, 2009.

Stuart Brown Ted lecture, online at http://blog.ted. com/2009/03/12/stuart_brown_play.

Daena Giardella, www.daenagiardella.com.

Embracing the Elephant —
Make way for your new future!

DO YOU HAVE AN elephant in *your* room? Most of us have at least one. As you might guess, the elephant is the subject we'd like to forget when thinking about our future. Perhaps it's because the subject is too personal, too confusing or just frightening.

Take the lady in the photo sitting comfortably on the sofa while ignoring the huge pachyderm. She'll have a problem if "Pachy" moves, is hungry or wants to sit in her seat — upsetting her status quo.

The second half of life is not about the status quo. It's about change within us and our environment.

Ask yourself:

- What are the elephants in my room as I look to the future?

- What concerns seem easier to avoid than address?

In planning for the next chapter of life, people typically avoid three subjects — ageism, sex and death — in no particular order. Consider the following questions:

- Ageism: What is it and what can I do about it?

- Sex: Do you mean older people do it?

- Death: How can this be a non-taboo subject for me?

Ageism: What is it?

"Ageism creates needless fear, waste, illness and misery especially among older people. It is a social disease much like racism and sexism."
— Erdman Palmore, professor emeritus, Department
of Sociology, Duke University, Durham, NC

The term "ageism" was coined in 1968 by the late pioneer in aging, Dr. Robert N. Butler, Pulitzer Prize winner, founding director of the National Institute on Aging and CEO of the International Longevity Center USA. Ageism is prejudice against older people. It is systematic discrimination based on chronological age and often is used to define capabilities and roles.

Ageism is subtle yet pervasive. A 2001 Duke University survey found that 80 percent of Americans 60 and older experienced some form of age discrimination. Thirty-one percent said they were regularly ignored or not taken seriously because of their age.

> *"Ageism is more than images, words, actions and attitudes.*
> *It is deeply embedded in society ... "*
> —*Robert N. Butler,* "Ageism: Looking Back over My Shoulder,"
> *Generations, Fall 2000*

Here are a few examples:

- The caregiver for a successful and autocratic 92-year-old businessman suffering from lung cancer, routinely referred to him as "sweetie" and "just adorable." Kristine Williams, a nurse gerontologist and associate professor at the University of Kansas School of Nursing, believes that such infantilizing comments tell older adults that they are incompetent.

- A nonprofit organization needed a new chairperson for the membership committee. A board member suggested that the search committee find a "young, energetic and creative person who can get things done." The board president countered, "How about a middle age or older person who is energetic, creative and can get things done?" There was silence in the room.

- A speaker finished delivering a dynamic speech to a group of about 300 people when someone from the audience asked her age. She told them, "70." Several in the audience re-marked, "You look great for your age." The speaker thanked them and asked with a smile, "How did you expect me to look?" She was tempted to use a variation of the Gloria Steinman line by saying, "This is what 70 looks like," but didn't.

- Finally, we have the issue of age discrimination in the work-place. According to the Federal Age Discrimination in Employment Act, decisions of employment, termination, training and benefits cannot be based solely on age for most jobs for individuals 40 and older. Consequently, employ-ers usually are cautious in expressing age-biased remarks.

Instead, code phrases often are used. For example, mature job seekers report being told, "You are over-qualified" which may be code for "you're too old."

Why does ageism occur?

Prejudice against older people has roots in our cultural values. We are a youth-oriented society that perpetuates age stereotypes that underlie age biases in decisions and attitudes. Just look at commercial advertising, fashion photography and television sitcoms. Youth is portrayed as attractive, strong and potent, fast, productive and innovative. The assumption is that if you aren't young… you therefore are not attractive, strong, potent, fast, productive or innovative.*

Second, hiring managers and other decision makers are generally uninformed about aging and often make assumptions about what an older person can and cannot do based on age. Decision makers in corporations, universities, religious institutions and volunteer organizations could improve their knowledge about normal aging, performance and potential.

Third, age stereotypes provide a framework for clarity, helping to bring order to a complex, unpredictable and rather disorganized world, even though it's based on prejudicial thinking.** In ambiguous situations, it's even more likely that individuals revert to stereotypes to remove uncertainties. Blaming older Americans who receive Social Security and Medicare for the U.S. deficit is an example.

Are we sensitive or just lacking a sense of humor?

Birthday cards are a good example. At best, they are ambivalent and typically don't convey a positive attitude or image. While we

---

* Carnevale, A.P. & Stone, S.C. (1994). Developing the new competitive workforce. In J.D. Auerbach & J.D. Welsh (Eds.), *Aging and competition: Rebuilding the U.S. workforce.* pp.94-141.

** Montepare, J.M. & Zebrowitz, L.A. (2002). A social-development view of ageism. In T.D. Nelson (Ed.), *Ageism: Stereotyping and prejudice against older persons.* Cambridge, MA: A Bradford Book – MIT Press. Pp. 77-115.

can't take ourselves too seriously, repeated negative messages suggest it's socially acceptable to insult a person on his or her birthday. Sociologist Erdman Palmore's research found that certain types of stereotypes are dominant in birthday cards — lacking physical abilities, being unattractive, having no sexual interest or capacity and wanting to conceal our age. Let's add to that list the fear of losing mental abilities.

In looking at a few sample birthday cards, we found cards that encouraged recipients to celebrate by lifting their chins, tightening their lips and smiling because guess what? They just had a face-lift. Another showed an older man talking to another about the new sports car he bought. Instead of being thrilled, he was cranky. Why? He forgot where he parked the car. And then there's the one that illustrated an older woman telling police that someone has stolen everything in her car, including the steering wheel and dashboard. The police officer called in the report and then quickly cancelled it. The woman had gotten into the back seat of her car.

Yes, we laugh, but upon reflection, what is the message that's being sent to us — repeatedly?

Birthday cards for centenarians are different. They consistently convey positive recognition of this landmark birthday with glowing prose. One card reads, "100 years old and you are simply a wonderful woman, faithful friend, generous spirit, charming soul, compassionate being, etc." In 2007, Hallmark sold about 85,000 100th birthday cards. Perhaps one has to reach 100 to be praised.

Ageism is bad for your health

Becca Levy, associate professor of epidemiology and psychology at Yale University found that age insults can lead to health consequences. And little insults can lead to more negative images of aging. Her study revealed that those who had more of these negative images were less healthy and had lower survival rates. Other research by Levy found that people exposed to negative images of aging including words such as "forget," "feeble" and "shaky" performed significantly worse on memory and balance tests. They also showed higher levels of stress.

The good news is that those who had a positive view of aging lived, on average, 7.5 years longer than those with a negative view of aging. That was larger than increases associated with exercising or not smoking.

What can you do when encountering ageism?

- If you hear an ageist remark, ask for some clarification and offer some alternative language.

- If you feel you are the object of age discrimination in the workplace, speak to the human resources department as a beginning. To file a charge, go to the U.S. Equal Employment Opportunity Commission.

- If you see an advertisement portraying older adults in a negative way or they are absent in advertisements for fashion, cosmetics or cars, write to the publisher and the advertiser.

- Dispel the myths of ageism by your own presentation and behavior. Continue to learn, love, grow and contribute.

Why should we care? We live in a culture where individuals frequently make judgments and decisions that are influenced by our age instead of who we are, what we think and what we can do. Each of us needs to be a trailblazer to fight ageism. We and society will benefit.

According to the 2006 International Longevity Center (ILC) report "Ageism in America," "older Americans experience widespread mistreatment ranging from stereotypic and degrading media images to physical and financial abuse, unequal treatment in the workforce and denial of appropriate medical care and services."

Sex: Are Older People Doing It?

"Perhaps the ultimate manifestation of age prejudice is the extent to which older people are considered incapable of intimate sexual experience."
—Robert N. Butler in "Ageism: Looking Back over
My Shoulder," published in Generations, Fall 2005.

In their book *The New Love and Sex after 60*, the late Robert N. Butler and Myrna I. Lewis wrote that attitudes about sexuality have been shaped by our genes, parents, families, teachers and society. Some of these attitudes are positive. Others are negative and many of which we are unaware.

Myths about sex or sexuality in later life occur for many reasons:

▓ Folklore has shaped some of our attitudes. For example, idealized figures such as grandmothers baking cookies and grandfathers in their rocking chairs are not supposed to have sex lives.

▓ Many fear growing old and death.

▓ Men have placed excessive emphasis on life-long physical performance. Butler and Lewis write that men judge themselves by comparing their sexual performance with that of younger men. Also, women may see themselves as unattractive as they become less firm and have wrinkles and graying hair.

Take the following true-false myths quiz to learn more facts about age and sexuality.

1. **Frequency of sexual activity significantly declines for active adults in their early 50s to the early 70s.**

False. Data from the University of Chicago's National Social Life, Health and Aging Project, described as the first comprehensive national survey of senior sexual attitudes, behaviors and problems, found that sexual activity declined only slightly. Additionally, most people 58 to 85 thought that sexuality was an important part of life.

2. **We know a great deal about how sexual activities and functions change as people age.**

False. Researcher Dr. Stacy Tessler Lindau of the University of Chicago reports that we are lacking reliable information about how sexual activity and function might change with age, illness and the taboos — all of which contribute to worry and even shame among many older adults.

3. **Drugs for erectile dysfunction are aphrodisiacs used to sustain problem relationships.**

False. If the problem is intimacy, such drugs typically are not the solution; they do not repair damaged relationships. However, they do increase the likelihood of an erection.

4. **Older adults typically are reluctant to answer questions about sex.**

False. In 2005 and 2006, researchers from the University of Chicago interviewed over 3,000 people age 57 to 85 in their homes. Only between two percent and seven percent declined to answer questions about their sexual activities. Study participants were more likely to refuse questions about income than they were about sex.

5. **Age is a better indicator than health for many aspects of sexuality.**

False. Health actually is a better indicator for sexuality. The most common reason for sexual inactivity among those with a spouse or partner was the male partner's physical health. Women not in a current relationship were more likely than men to report a lack of interest.

6. The second language of sex is learned rather than instinctive.

True. Sex is not just a matter of "athletics and production." The second language of sex is emotional and communicative as well as physical — and often is underdeveloped. One learns to recognize and share feelings in words, actions and "unspoken perceptions." The second language of sex is an aptitude that is acquired over time from the experience of giving and receiving.

7. There is such a thing as male menopause.

True. According to the Mayo Clinic, the term "male menopause" or "andropause" is sometimes used to describe the decreasing levels of testosterone related to men's aging. Note that female menopause is quite different. In women, ovulation ends and hormone production dramatically declines during a short period of time. In men, the decline of testosterone is more gradual. Losses in energy level and mood changes tend to be more subtle for men and might not be noticed for years.

8. The main reason that women do not engage in sexual activities is that they don't have a partner.

True. Women have longer life expectancies and lower rates of re-marriage after widowhood. This is considered a demographic dilemma. However, women adapt. They build new friendships, establish relationships with younger men and sublimate their sexuality by engaging in absorbing activities that lead to accomplishment and companionship. **

9. The late Kitty Carlisle, singer, actress and wife of playwright Moss Hart, made her nightclub debut in New York at age 94.

---

* Butler, R.N and Lewis, M. (2002) *The New Love and Sex after 60*, Ballantine Books.

** *Ibid.*

True. Gail Sheehy, in her book *Sex and the Seasoned Woman,* tells the story of Ms. Carlisle being paid $20,000 to get up on a table every night and sing in Palm Beach. She also performed to sold-out audiences at the Regency Hotel on Park Avenue in New York. When asked, "What do old men need?" Carlisle replied, "The same thing younger men need. The same thing all men need — someone to listen to them. And I'm a very good listener."

10. **The need to be touched is life-long.**

True. We never outgrow the need for touch. It's important to consider cultural differences as well as the appropriateness and the meaning of touching another person. Intimacy, love and attachment are timeless and vital to the well-being of older people.

Death (or End of Life): Is This Taboo for Me?

Dying is a natural part of our existence, yet our culture is unique in that death is viewed as a taboo subject. When someone dies, we use euphemisms such as the deceased is "no longer with us," has "passed," "gone to meet his or her maker" or "kicked the bucket."

We lack personal experience with death, which just adds to our fear and trepidation. Most people don't die at home but in hospitals and other health care facilities. In 2007, 6,500 individuals died daily in the U.S. — only 1,200 died at home. Death has been removed as a common experience.

Three aspects important to face

The first aspect is the emotional preparation to realize our own mortality. The issue is not "if" but rather "when." Knowing that time is precious and fleeting can serve as a positive motivator to make every day count.

In 2005, the late Steve Jobs, then CEO of Apple, gave the commencement speech at Stanford University. He said that at 17, he remembered reading a quote "that went something like this: 'If you live each day as if it was your last, someday you'll most certainly be right.' It made an impression on me, and since then, for the past 33 years, I have looked in the mirror every morning and asked myself: 'If today were the last day of my life, would I want to do what I am about to do today?' And whenever the answer has been 'no' for too many days in a row, I know I need to change something."

We live in a unique time with increased life expectancy and medical advances that have defeated many sudden causes of death such as heart attacks and strokes. We now are dying of what has been called incremental or slow moving illnesses such as cardiovascular disease, cancer, respiratory illnesses and diabetes. That means we have more time and ability to shape how we want to exit the planet.

It's a time when we can document our wishes, address personal issues of saying goodbye, make amends and get in touch with the spiritual side of life. It also reminds us of the gift of time.

Here's an exercise for you:

Compare the two lists. Identify those most important to you... and "just do it."

What would I do with my life if knew I would live forever?

1.

2.

3.

4.

5.

What would I do if I knew I had just one year to live?

1.

2.

3.

4.

5.

The second aspect of addressing end-of-life issues involves the practical tasks of completing a Power of Attorney for Health Care, a Power of Attorney for Financial Matters, an estate plan, a plan for long-term care and a plan for funeral and burial. (See the chapter on "Your Wishes Matter.")

The third aspect is the important conversation with family members and close friends. This may be the most difficult part of end-of-life planning. Here's a familiar situation: A parent wants to initiate the conversation with adult children and is met with the response, "Oh Mom (or Dad), you're going to outlive all of us — no need to talk about that now."

People have many reasons for resisting the dialogue. Some believe that talking about death will bring it on. Adult children may avoid facing the fact that their parents are going to die at some point. The imagined loss may feel unbearable; it's easier not to think about it. For others, family conflict, jealousy, greed and unsolved family riffs are barriers to the important conversation. That does not mean the conversation should be avoided.

So where to begin?

Joyce Cavanaugh, Texas A & M Associate Professor and Extension Family Economics Specialist, provides several useful points for discussion on end-of-life issues:*

- It's important to let others know you want to be taken seriously. Suggested opener: "I want to talk to you about something that is important to me. I hope you are willing to listen."

- Refer to a past situation of a terminally ill friend or a story in the news such as Terri Schiavo. Suggested opener: "Remember what happened to Mary after her stroke? I don't want that to happen to me."

---

* Cavanaugh, J. (April 2005). *Talking to Your Family about End-of-Life Issues*, Texas AgriLife Extension Service. Retrieved October 26, 2011 http://fcs.tamu. edu/money/your_money/money_pdfs/talking_to_your_family.pdf

■ Tell your family member(s) or close friend(s) whom you have chosen as your health care agent. Explain that this person will be responsible for helping make the medical team understand your wishes about a terminal illness and other issues. To avoid conflict, relate your feelings to all of your family members.

■ Timing is important. Select a time when your family is together so they hear the same thing at the same time. If this is not possible, meet with family members individually or in small groups.

■ Select a time that is not a celebration or special holiday.

■ If possible, select a time when the family is well rested and alert. This is likely to be an emotionally draining conversation for some.

Your legacy

How do you want to be remembered? What do you want your family to remember about you? One way is to write an ethical will. Consider it a voice of the heart or a love letter to your family. It's also an excellent way to gain clarity for yourself.

Here are some common themes: your personal values and beliefs, important spiritual values, blessings and hopes for future generations, lessons you have learned, forgiving others and asking to be forgiven. (See the chapter on "Living in 3D.")

The following two guides are extremely useful for those difficult yet important conversations. They are personal and address the "what if" situations. They are caring, compassionate, comprehensive and practical.

✓ **The Good to Go Toolkit.** This 16-page resource is designed to help you identify priorities and ensure that your wishes are honored. The material is designed to guide you through the process of making and communicating your decisions. It begins with a Values Worksheet that can be shared with your loved ones and physician as well as wishes for therapies that could sustain life.

✓ **Your Way ... With a Little Help from Your Friends.** This guide helps you stay in charge of your medical care. The 12-page tool is useful if you become ill and can't tell medical professionals what you want. It asks important questions about what matters to you most, envisioning possible situations as well as life, death and pain management. Criteria for identifying that special friend to manage and honor your requests is included.

Conclusion to LIVE SMART AFTER 50!

The Experts' Guide to Life Planning for Uncertain Times

Although we will never have total control over our lives, we have the opportunity to make choices that influence how we age and live our later years. We must know what's important to us, and act on that awareness and knowledge. Self-reliance is the theme. And that includes a strong relationship with our communities. No individual, employer or government agency will create the lifestyle or make the decisions for us that will make the next chapter of our life the best chapter. That's up to us.

A few points to remember:

- Our social, political and economic environment makes it imperative for each of us to take charge of our own lives and live smart.

- We likely will live 20, 30 or even 40 years after our first job or career. Yes, living to be 100 is a real possibility and we need to plan for it.

- We may be working longer than we thought.

- We live in a time of uncertainty. Doing everything "right" at work, with our family and in our community is no longer a guarantee that our lives will evolve in a predictable manner.

- We have the opportunity to maximize our physical, mental and creative capacities. Growth is part of aging.

- Flexibility is key. We need to be ready to modify and integrate the different aspects of life at any time, even with a plan. Our health, financial security, relationships, living arrangements and care for family members are part of the dynamic mix that goes with living a full and responsible life.

- To increase the chances of living the life we want, each of us must have an intention — a plan — that reflects our priorities, realities, dreams and opportunities. As is evident from the various chapters in this book, living the life we want requires a holistic plan that addresses the subject that each chapter discusses — at a minimum. Our lives combine the individual parts into a whole, making us who we are and what we want to become.

- At any age, security, health and fulfillment are important. They become even more important as we age. Be certain to add some joy and fun for good measure. As stated from an unknown source, "The journey of life is long (if we are lucky), so take lots of snacks and magazines."

- The best news is that (almost) all is possible. This book — along with information from other reliable sources and the added value of skilled professionals — can help guide us through a new life stage. This new gift of time allows us to make informed choices, seize opportunities, grow as individuals and contribute to our communities.

Move the elephant(s) out of the room…
make informed decisions…
and grab hold of the brass ring and fly!

Life Planning Network Chapter Contributor

Helen Dennis, MA, Specialist in aging, employment and the new retirement, Co-author of *Project Renewment: The First Retirement Model for Career Women.*

Resources

Ageism

Equal Employment Opportunity Commission, www.eeoc.gov/laws/types/age.cfm.

Margaret Morganroth Gullette, *Agewise: Fighting the New Ageism in America,* University of Chicago Press, 2011.

Todd D. Nelson (editor), *Ageism: Stereotyping and Prejudice Against Older Persons,* MIT Press, 2002.

Erdman B. Palmore, *Ageism: Negative and Positive,* Springer Publishing Co., 1999.

Sex (Sexuality)

Boston Women's Health Book Collective. *Our Bodies, Ourselves.* Simon & Schuster, 2011 (See chapters on Sexual Health and Our Later Years).

Bernice Bratter and Helen Dennis, *Project Renewment: The First Retirement Model for Career Women,* Scribner, 2008 (Essay on "Sex: Lest we Forget").

Robert N. Butler and Myrna I. Lewis, *The New Love and Sex after 60,* Ballantine Books, 2002.

Jane Fonda, *Prime Time: Love, Health, Sex, Fitness, Friendship, Spirit, Making the Most of All of Your Life,* Random House, 2011.

Gail Sheehy, *Sex and the Seasoned Woman,* Random House, 2006.

Sexual Health and Aging: Keeping the Passion Alive, Mayo Clinic, www.mayoclinic.com/health/sexual-health/HA00035.

End of life

Bernice Bratter and Helen Dennis, *Project Renewment: The First Retirement Model for Career Women,* Scribner, 2008 (Essay on "Who Will Be There for Me?").

The Good to Go Toolkit, http://community.compassionandchoices. org/document.doc?id=425.

Healthcare Elder Law Programs, Inc., www.help4srs.org.

Elisabeth Kűbler-Ross, *On Death and Dying,* Touchstone - Simon & Schuster, 1997.

Elisabeth Kűbler-Ross and David Kessler, *Life Lessons,* Touchstone, 2000.

Your Way... With a Little Help from Your Friends, www.help4srs. org/node/230.

Zalmon Schacter-Shalom, From Age-ing to Sage-ing: A Profound New Vision of Growing Older, Warner Books, 1995.

Appendix A —
Lifeline Exercise

Lifeline Exercise Instructions

BEGIN WITH AN 8½" × 11" SHEET OF PAPER.

Draw a line across the middle of the page, from left to right. You may choose to segment the line in ten year increments so that you have a clearer picture of the times in your life. This is your lifeline.

Next, mark an "X" where you are today on your lifeline. For example, if you decide you are midway through your life, put the "X" in the middle of the line.

Now begin to review your life to date. Consider within your lifeline's ten year increments the significant events in your life. Place your happiest moments and, in your eyes, your most successful moments above the line, and place your unhappy moments and "failure" moments below the line. The happier the moment, the higher it goes above the line and the unhappier the moment, the lower it goes below the line.

Don't try to create an exhaustive list, just capture the most significant experiences in your life. Some triggers for your memory: education, career, marriage, children, grandchildren, family changes (death, illness, divorce), moves, travel / vacations, mentors / teachers, accomplishments, role of music / art / literature, religious / spiritual experiences, politics, hobbies / sports, financial changes, your health, etc.

BIRTHDATE

As you review your lifeline, write down your answers to these four questions.

1. Do you see patterns or recurring themes in your lifeline? Patterns may tell you something about what your life has been about, as well as what's most important to you.

2. What were your happiest and most successful times and what were your unhappiest or least successful times? What do those ups and downs represent to you? Do you see a theme? Often what we learn here can be clues to our values, gifts and passions. Next ask yourself, how can you enable more of the happiest or successful times in the future?

3. What were the two or three most important learning experiences in your life? What preceded them? Were they associated with a crisis, transition, confrontation or unexpected challenge? This will tell you something about how you adapt to and learn from adversity and transitions, and how you will deal with challenges as you age.

4. Where did you put your "X"? How much of your life is still ahead of you? Are there things you haven't done, but want to? What are they? Have you created a plan to make them happen?

Common themes in my life:

_____

_____

_____

Appendix B—
Relationship Assessment Worksheet

CHOOSE FOUR PEOPLE who are important in your life. List their names at the top of the sheet. Then respond to each question for each person, according to the letter you assigned them to above.

After completing all the questions for each person, answer the three questions at the end of the exercise.

Names: A_____ B_____ C_____ D_____

We enjoy mutual trust, understanding and respect for each other

A ○ Usually ○ Sometimes ○ Rarely

B ○ Usually ○ Sometimes ○ Rarely

C ○ Usually ○ Sometimes ○ Rarely

D ○ Usually ○ Sometimes ○ Rarely

We both feel heard, appreciated and supported

A ○ Usually ○ Sometimes ○ Rarely

B ○ Usually ○ Sometimes ○ Rarely

C ○ Usually ○ Sometimes ○ Rarely

D ○ Usually ○ Sometimes ○ Rarely

We are able to raise difficult issues with one another

A ○ Usually ○ Sometimes ○ Rarely

B ○ Usually ○ Sometimes ○ Rarely

C ○ Usually ○ Sometimes ○ Rarely

D ○ Usually ○ Sometimes ○ Rarely

We each take responsibility for our actions and do not blame one other

A ○ Usually ○ Sometimes ○ Rarely

B ○ Usually ○ Sometimes ○ Rarely

C ○ Usually ○ Sometimes ○ Rarely

D ○ Usually ○ Sometimes ○ Rarely

We both enjoy the time we spend together

A ○ Usually ○ Sometimes ○ Rarely

B ○ Usually ○ Sometimes ○ Rarely

C ○ Usually ○ Sometimes ○ Rarely

D ○ Usually ○ Sometimes ○ Rarely

We actively resolve our differences or agree to disagree

A ○ Usually ○ Sometimes ○ Rarely

B ○ Usually ○ Sometimes ○ Rarely

C ○ Usually ○ Sometimes ○ Rarely

D ○ Usually ○ Sometimes ○ Rarely

We share some similar interests

A ○ Usually ○ Sometimes ○ Rarely

B ○ Usually ○ Sometimes ○ Rarely

C ○ Usually ○ Sometimes ○ Rarely

D ○ Usually ○ Sometimes ○ Rarely

We both put energy into maintaining the relationship

A   ○ Usually   ○ Sometimes   ○ Rarely

B   ○ Usually   ○ Sometimes   ○ Rarely

C   ○ Usually   ○ Sometimes   ○ Rarely

D   ○ Usually   ○ Sometimes   ○ Rarely

We both feel physically and emotionally safe in the relationship

A   ○ Usually   ○ Sometimes   ○ Rarely

B   ○ Usually   ○ Sometimes   ○ Rarely

C   ○ Usually   ○ Sometimes   ○ Rarely

D   ○ Usually   ○ Sometimes   ○ Rarely

We have many values in common

A   ○ Usually   ○ Sometimes   ○ Rarely

B   ○ Usually   ○ Sometimes   ○ Rarely

C   ○ Usually   ○ Sometimes   ○ Rarely

D   ○ Usually   ○ Sometimes   ○ Rarely

---

1. Which relationships are currently the healthiest and feel most supportive?

2. Which relationships are currently in need of work? What are some of the changes you plan to make?

3. What are the most important changes you can make in your key relationships?

Appendix C—
Clarifying Housing and Community Preferences

WHEN CONSIDERING YOUR POTENTIAL future housing options and the community where you may reside, you face many choices. Living smart by making good decisions involves answering questions such as: Where do I want to be? Who do I want to live with and/or be near? What are the key elements I want or need in my home and community? You also need to be aware of the values that color your preferences. This checklist can serve as a starting point for clarifying the kind of housing and community you want to move toward. When you have completed the exercise, share it with family or friends, and identify new questions that move you even closer to making these major decisions.

Use the boxes to the right of each item to rate how important that factor is to you as you consider your future home. Check the box under the number that most closely corresponds to that item's importance to you, using the following scale:

1. **Not at all important**

2. **Somewhat unimportant**

3. **I'm neutral**

4. **Somewhat important**

5. **Extremely important**

My Next Home and Community

Geographic aspects of my community	1	2	3	4	5
Coastal setting					
Mountain setting					
Desert setting					
Forest setting					
Valley setting					
Other:					
Climate preferences	**1**	**2**	**3**	**4**	**5**
Changing seasons					
Moderate temperature and seasonal changes					
Hot and arid					
Tropical					
Lots of snow					
Other:					
Location of my community	**1**	**2**	**3**	**4**	**5**
Near walking trails and bike paths					
Walking distance to places I frequent					
Has easy-to-use transportation system					
Has easy access for those with disabilities					
Exists in an urban setting					
Exists in a suburban setting					
Exists in a rural, sparsely populated setting					
Near a major airport					
Near my job or places where I could be employed					
Near a college or university					
Near arts and culture					
Near my religious institution					
Near good shopping and restaurants					
Is in a very safe area					

Is in a very affordable area					
Other:					
Health and support services	**1**	**2**	**3**	**4**	**5**
Is located near a hospital					
Has a public health clinic					
Has fitness/recreation facilities					
Offers home-based assistance for aging in place (Meals On Wheels, home modification services, a "village" organization, etc.)					
Has community wellness programs					
Has senior-friendly features (well marked pedestrian crossings, readable street signs, benches, etc.)					
Has affordable door-to-curb transportation for those who can't drive					
Other:					
Social/Spiritual Resources	**1**	**2**	**3**	**4**	**5**
Is near immediate family members					
Offers home-sharing with friend for social and economic support					
Is near my "tribe"—those with whom I share similar interests					
Includes mostly people my own age					
Includes a variety of generations and ages					
Includes the friends I have today					
Includes cultural diversity					
Other:					
Housing type	**1**	**2**	**3**	**4**	**5**
Single family home					
Multi-family home (duplex, apartment)					
Mobile home					
Town home					
Co-Housing community					
Active adult community					

	1	2	3	4	5
Independent/assisted living community					
Continuous Care Retirement Community (CCRC)					
Other:					
Home/physical space	**1**	**2**	**3**	**4**	**5**
Has outdoor space (patio or deck or garden, etc.)					
Has privacy					
Outside is maintained by property management					
Has garage					
Has ample storage space					
Includes space for overnight guests					
Has Universal Design elements — curbless entry showers, wider doorways, lower countertops, etc.					
Is ready "as is" — needs no major repairs or modifications					
Has a full kitchen					
Other:					
Costs — relative to my current residence	**1**	**2**	**3**	**4**	**5**
Monthly rent or mortgage					
Utilities (water, electricity, gas, trash removal, lawn maintenance, cable, phone, etc.)					
Taxes					
Additional Services					
Other:					
Inheritability — an asset I can leave to family					

Appendix D—
Goals and Major Expenditures in Your Second Half of Life

A Timeline

THINK ABOUT EACH AREA BELOW. If you have a goal or intent related to the category, list it in the appropriate box under the time frame that you would like this to occur. If it has a dollar ($) cost, include the dollar ($) cost. Also include any major expenditures that are not frequent or recurring, but may be necessary, such as a new car, roof repair, house painting, etc. After you make your list, prioritize the items by numbering them in order of importance to you. (You won't have something in every box—just where you have a goal or expense coming up.)

Total the amounts for each time frame. These are funds in addition to your regular expenses that you will need to either save for or earmark funds towards. You may find that you'll need to reduce your regular spending in order to have the funds for the goals and major expenditures on this list. Use this in your conversation with your financial planner.

Goals For Your Life

Free yourself™

Name: _____ **Date:** _____

	1-12 Months	2-3 Years	4-5 Years	6-10 Years	11-20 Years	Lifetime
Family/ Relationships						
Home/ Environment						
Leisure/Toys/ Recreation						
Education/ Personal Development						
Work/ Career						
Charitable/ Gifting						
Community/ Spiritual						
Other:						

RTD Financial Advisors (Atlanta, Philadelphia) (800) 893-4725
Adapted from George Kinder, CFP®, The Kinder Institute of Life Planning

Appendix E —
The Core Financial Pieces for a Thriving Second Half of Life Worksheet

THIS PROCESS AND WORKSHEET will help you develop a more complete picture and understanding of your financial situation and will prepare you well for working with your chosen financial planner. As you gather your information together, list the individual components or resources and the questions you have or feelings you experience as you think about the pieces. Attach copies of your statements, policies and titles, etc. as you compile this information.

Sources of Income — These might include pensions, social security, earned income, dividend and interest, rental income, etc.

Item	Description/Notes (Account Number, etc.)	Value

Questions and feelings I experience as I think about this area:

Relevant Documents

- Income tax returns for the last three years
- Two most recent pay stubs
- Social security statements
- Pension statements
- Deferred compensation arrangements
- Other statements of income (rental, annuity, trust, etc.)

Liquid Assets/Emergency Cash Reserves — A liquid asset is cash that is readily available or an investment that can easily be turned into cash, which in the words of the great Yogi Berra "is just as good as money!" This includes bank deposits, CDs, short-term bonds and money market accounts. It does not include the checking account you use to pay bills. Cash reserves represent your "Emergency Fund" for life's little emergencies. Ideally you should have three to six months of your living expenses set aside, even in retirement.

Item	Description/Notes (Account Number, etc.)	Value

Questions and feelings I experience as I think about this area:

Relevant Documents

- Checking accounts
- Savings accounts
- Money market accounts
- CDs
- Savings bonds

Investment Assets — This is money beyond your Emergency Reserves for your future use. It can include stocks, bonds, mutual funds, Exchange Traded Funds, real estate, collectibles, land, etc. You will draw on these accounts to supplement your sources of income in order to support your quality of life.

Item	Description/Notes (Account Number, etc.)	Value

Questions and feelings I experience as I think about this area:

Relevant Documents

- Brokerage and mutual fund accounts
- Stock options
- Restricted stock plans
- Other investment accounts
- Employer sponsored retirement plans (401k, 403b, 457, SEP, SIMPLE, etc.)
- Traditional IRA accounts
- Roth IRA accounts
- IRA Custodial Agreements
- Employer Retirement Plan Document / Summary Plan description
- 529, Coverdell ESA, UTMA/UGMA savings

Home—Understanding your home's role in your life and its value, financially and emotionally, is important. Your home may be your castle or your nest or an albatross. It may be more than you need or want at this point or it may be ideal. If it doesn't meet your needs, can you sell it for enough money to buy something you want? Do you owe more than it's worth due to the slowdown in the economy? Does the house require a lot of maintenance and repair that could strain your budget? Is it located in a desirable area for meeting your needs socially, in terms of safety and access to meaningful services?

Item	Description/Notes	Value

Questions and feelings I experience as I think about this area:

Relevant Documents

- Property appraisals
- Property tax documents

Consumer Debts/Short Term Liabilities — These are the debts we incur usually when we are spending without planning, that is, living beyond our means or letting lifestyle purchases become longtime debts. Credit cards and revolving store credit cards are examples. Car loans are considered short term loans. Some debt may be unavoidable but debt payments limit our freedom, absorb money that could go to savings or a quality lifestyle or reserves. As you prepare for the second half of life, reducing debt will make a huge difference in the stability of your financial life and give you more choices.

Item	Description/Notes	Value

Questions and feelings I experience as I think about this area:

Relevant Documents

- Credit reports
- Credit card statements
- Auto loan statements
- Student loan statements

Long-term liabilities — These are debts on life assets that may make sense but need to be tracked and that can place more pressure on our ability to live well within our means, particularly once we are no longer working. Your home mortgage, equity lines of credit or mortgages on other real estate, on business or education loans are types of long-term liabilities. Do you have opportunities to refinance and reduce your interest costs? Can you pay off a loan before you stop working? Can you manage the debt when you stop working? Do you still want that asset or could you sell it?

Item	Description/Notes (Account Number, etc.)	Value

Questions and feelings I experience as I think about this area:

Relevant Documents

- Mortgage and home equity loan/line of credit statements
- Other business or personal debt statements

Life Assets — These are items that don't necessarily represent a valuable financial asset but they have meaning to you. A life asset may also be a financial asset that you happen to also love, such as your home, a vacation home, your cars, art work and collectibles. A life asset might also be memorabilia that has no financial value but has heart or emotional value. It may also include furnishings, recreational equipment, hobby supplies, jewelry or clothes, if these are items that have meaning to you. An asset only goes here if it really adds meaning to your life. We need to assess them because, unless we are Bill Gates, we generally can't afford to have all of the life assets we dream about. That's okay. What really matters to you?

Item	Description/Notes	Value

Questions and feelings I experience as I think about this area:

Relevant Documents

- Titles of ownership

Stuff and Junk — These are assets that may now be more of a burden than a value. Things we no longer use or need, that take up space. It's wonderful to identify the pieces that no longer belong in our puzzle!

Item	Description/Notes	Value

Questions and feelings I experience as I think about this area:

Risk Management Protections — Typically in the form of insurance, these protections replace the things or the income or the assets that we could lose as a result of disaster, accident, ill health, long-term illness or death. This is at the core of building a financial foundation — having protections in place. Health insurance and long-term care insurance are particularly important as we age. While the costs of insurance can be high, the cost of being unprotected can be catastrophic. Gather your statements and policies and review. Your advisor will help you if you are concerned about having adequate protection as you age.

Item	Description/Notes (Policy Number, etc.)	Value

Questions and feelings I experience as I think about this area:

Relevant Documents

- Annuity contracts
- Life insurance policies
- Health/dental/vision insurance policies
- Medicare supplement policies
- Disability insurance policies

- Auto insurance policies
- Homeowner/renter's insurance policies
- Umbrella liability policies
- Long-term care policies
- Professional liability policies
- Other insurance
- Wills
- Trust documents
- Powers of attorney
- Living will
- Employee benefits booklets
- Partnership and buy/sell agreements
- Pre/Post-nuptial agreements
- Beneficiary forms

Appendix F—
Money Workbook

My Financial Circumstances

Tips adapted from veteran financial planner, Ben Coombs, CFP®

COMPLETE THE CONCISE FINANCIAL STATEMENT in the following worksheet to help you evaluate the adequacy of your savings and investments to supplement other sources of retirement income and maintain your current lifestyle as you grow older. This snapshot of your financial circumstances will address the core components of your financial well-being—now and in the future. For additional information and supplemental instructions, see the corresponding steps below the worksheet.

Worksheet

Step 1	Enter the total value of your savings and investments as of (enter date) _____	$
Step 2	Enter the estimated total of your annual expenses for the last 12 months.	$
Step 3	Enter your total annual income minus any investment income you realize.	$
Step 4	Subtract the total for Step 3 from the total of Step 2. This is the amount of income you will have to receive annually from your investments to supplement other sources of retirement income.	$
Step 5	Divide the total of Step 4 by the total of Step 1. This is the percentage rate your investments will need to earn (ignoring inflation) in order to adequately supplement your other sources of retirement income.	_____%
Step 6	Consult with a Certified Financial Planner™ and Life Planner to integrate all the elements of your life and financial resources and devise a living plan. (See Resources at the end of this chapter)	

Step 1: Enter the total value of your savings and investment accounts in the worksheet above. You can pull these figures from your last monthly bank, mutual fund and investment account statements.

Step 2: Tabulate what you spend on a monthly basis for fixed expenses, monthly and periodically. To this figure add your variable expenses, both those that occur monthly and those that are periodic. The point here is that you have more or less a steady monthly spending amount that includes fixed expenses and some variable expenses. You also have periodic expenses, such as quarterly pest control or landscaping, vacation, dues, etc. Total your monthly and periodic expenses to come up with a TOTAL ANNUAL SPENDING AMOUNT.

Step 3: Add up all of your sources of income except for earnings on investments. Include Social Security, any pensions, earned income, etc. If you are not currently drawing Social Security or pension benefits, request an estimate of what your benefits will be and add this to your total. The amount of income from these sources will generally depend on the age at which you begin to take benefits.

Step 4: Subtract the total annual income figure from the total annual expense figure. Record the remainder, which is the amount of income that your investments will have to supplement your other sources of income in order for you to maintain your current lifestyle.

Step 5: Divide the net amount of your annual expenses (Step 4) by the total value of your investments (Step 1). The answer will be the percent (%) your investment will have to earn each year (ignoring inflation) to support your current lifestyle. If this figure exceeds 4–4.5% then you may be depending too much on your investments to cover your future needs and will need to consider:

- Reducing your lifestyle costs

- Postponing retirement

- Working some amount in "retirement"

- Saving more money

- Postponing Social Security benefits (the monthly benefit will be higher the longer you postpone benefits, up to age 70)

- Taking more investment risk, with the guidance of a financial planning professional

- Prioritizing your lifestyle spending and consider again what matters most to you. A financial life planner can help you integrate all aspects of your financial and personal life as it is presented in this e-book so that you make the most of your financial resources in the context of who you are, what matters to you and how you want to live in the second half of your life.

Step 6: Consult with a qualified Certified Financial Planner (CFP) to review not only your calculations and your investments, but also all aspects of your financial life such as cash flow, insurance, future health care and housing, taxes and legacy planning. A qualified financial planner can help you think creatively and run what-if scenarios to help you arrive at a plan of action that will allow you to thrive and still protect your future.

Appendix G—
Home to Me Is...

BELOW ARE SOME QUESTIONS that can help you to identify your sense of place — the meaning of home for you. If you live with a spouse or partner, you may both wish to answer the questions. Jot notes in the book or on separate paper, or open a document on your computer to respond to each question

Past sense of "home": What positive associations do I have about "home" from my past, prior to where I live now? Where else have I felt "at home"? What was that like and with what and whom do I associate those subtle bonds?

Present home: What are my favorite spaces in my current home? Where do I curl up to read? Tackle projects? Where do I go when I need sanctuary? Where do I share a cup of tea with a friend? Where have the happy memories been forged?

Favorite rooms: What do I love about my favorite room in my house? What are my favorite memories based in this room? What different functions has this room served? How do I enjoy spending time there? If I knew I was going to be in this home another 10 or 15 years, what changes would I want to make?

Eyes of a stranger: Looking around my home as if for the first time, what do I see? What do the grounds tell me about the occupants? What does the exterior façade say about me or us? What do the pictures on the walls and the decorative items tell me? What pieces of furniture seem to have stories to tell? What do the piles of clutter indicate? What areas of this home make me feel happy? What areas feel uncomfortable?

Community: What do I like about my neighborhood? How has it served me? Who have been my friends here over the years? How do I define my community? Is it the town I live in, or perhaps the church I attend? Who are the members of "my tribe"? What do I like best about my community?

Review your responses to the above questions and then complete the following sentence:

Home to me is:

When you have completed this exercise, share your results and thoughts with your partner or a close friend. By completing the exercise and having conversations about it, you have begun to clarify what home means to you and how you may want to approach adapting your current home or creating your next home. You can explore many options as you search for the solution that best fits your needs, values, lifestyle and purse.

Appendix H —
Housing Transition Choices

OUR HOMES OFFER US a sense of family, security, comfort and independence. Sometimes housing choices become more complex as we age. This exercise gives you a way to think about options and make choices that preserve what's most important to you.

Housing Transitions	Best Choice	Second Best
In a situation where **My Health** prevents me from living safely and independently in my own home due to: • **Physical disabilities** (examples: walking up and down stairs, using the bathtub, reaching into cupboards, etc.) • **Cognitive disabilities** I would ...		
In a situation where I can **No Longer Drive**, I would ...		
In a situation where **My Spouse or Partner** is no longer with me (through death, separation or divorce), I would ...		
In a situation where I am **Retired** or no longer need to live close to my work, I would ...		
In a situation where **My Family* Moves** and no longer lives near me, I would ... * Family may be children, siblings, parents, or just those you care about		
In a situation where **My Finances** will no longer allow me to live in my current residence, I would ...		

When you have completed the exercise in contingency planning, share it with a trusted friend or family member, or a life planning professional. Talk about the choices you prefer to make and the second best options you would consider in each challenging scenario. Why do you prefer these options? What options would you not consider under any circumstances? Why not? Who might you seek out for guidance if one of these situations actually occurred in your later life?

Image Credits and Permissions

Page 25: Woman with Magnifying Glass: © Leung Cho Pan/ Dreamstime.com, used with permission.

Page 26: Federer: © anthonyshutterstock/bigstock.com, used with permission.

Page 26: Donald Trump: © Lev Radin/Shutterstock.com, used with permission.

Page 32: Sitting on the Solution Thumb: © David Spieth/ Dreamstime.com, used with permission.

Page 38: Relationship Diagram, used with permission.

Page 66: Carleen/The Steps Graphic, used with permission.

Page 71: Interior Decorator: © Lee Abel/LeeAbelPhotography. com, used with permission.

Page 73: Financial Consultant: © Lee Abel/LeeAbelPhotography. com, used with permission.

Page 74: Senior Center Director: © Lee Abel/LeeAbelPhotography. com, used with permission.

Page 74: Chef: © Lee Abel/LeeAbelPhotography.com, used with permission.

Page 96: Iceberg Model: reprinted with permission, from *Wellness Workbook*, 3rd edition, by John W. Travis, M.D. and Regina Sara Ryan (Celestial Arts, 2004), www.wellnessworkbook.

Page 119: Caregiving: used with permission from Family Caregiver Alliance.

Page 121: Leeza and Mom, used with permission.

Page 140: Compass Rose: © Darko Veselinovic/Fotolia, used with permission.

Page145: Footsteps: © Paulus Nugroho/Fotolia, used with permission.

Page 148: Spirituality: © Artellia/Dreamstime.com, used with permission.

Page 160: Sculptor: © Lee Abel/LeeAbelPhotography.com, used with permission.

Page 160: Chocolatier: © Lee Abel/ LeeAbelPhotography.com, used with permission.

Page 160: Painter: © Lee Abel/LeeAbelPhotography.com, used with permission.

Page 161: Seniors Running: © Marcelmooij/Dreamstime.com, used with permission.

Page 164: Life Story Theater: © Alan O'Hare, used with permission.

Page 169: Elephant in the Room: LPN, used with permission.

Page 98: Quotation on from *Pain Free: A Revolutionary Method for Stopping Chronic Pain* by Peter Egoscue used with permission of Random House/Bertelsmann.

Page 102: Quotation on from *Full Catastrophe Living* by Jon Kabat-Zinn used with permission of Random House/Bertelsmann.

CPSIA information can be obtained at www.ICGtesting.com
Printed in the USA
BVOW070323270613

324449BV00001B/1/P